Extraordinary
Asian Pacific Americans

By Susan Sinnott

Dedication

To Hsiao-Shan Chen, the Angel of Appleton,
whose diligence, good humor, and topsy-turvy life
I've admired for nearly twenty years. — S. S.

In loving memory of
my Dad, Dick Gway Yee (1914–1993),
who came to America — alone at the age of fifteen —
and found Gold Mountain deep within his heart.
With that, he taught his children that contentment
comes not from getting but in realizing. — L.D.

Extraordinary
Asian Pacific Americans

By Susan Sinnott

Consultants

S. E. Solberg, Ph.D., Executive Director,
American Institute for Humanities and Social Studies
University of Washington
Seattle, Washington

Brian Niiya
Asian American Studies Center
University of California, Los Angeles
Los Angeles, California

CHILDRENS PRESS ®
CHICAGO

Project editor: Alice Flanagan

Designer – illustrator – electronic page composition: Lindaanne Yee-Donohoe

Photo researcher: Carol Parden

Proofreader: Mark Friedman

Indexer: Schroeder Indexing Services

Engraver: Graphic Services

Printer: Lake Book Manufacturing, Inc.

Library of Congress Cataloging-in-Publication Data

Sinnott, Susan.
    Extraordinary Asian Pacific Americans/by Susan Sinnott
       p.   cm.
    Summary: Biographical sketches of notable Asian Amerians and Pacific Americans,
including cinematographer James Howe, scholar and politician S. I. Hayakawa, and
novelist Amy Tan.
    ISBN 0-516-03052-X
    1. Asian Americans — Biography — Juvenile literature. 2. Pacific Islander Americans —
Biography — Juvenile literature. [1. Asian Americans. 2. Pacific Islander Americans.]
I. Title.

E 184.06A38 1993   93 – 12678
920' .009295 — dc20   CIP
                                                      AC

CONTENTS

Asian Pacific American Immigration 9

Travelers to Gold Mountain 15

Chinese Railroad Workers 21

Yung Wing 24

Prisoners of Angel Island 29

Chinese Benevolent
Associations and Tongs 35

Polly Bemis (Lalu Nathoy) 39

The Chinese Laundry Business 43

Joe Shoong 46

Raising Sugarcane in Hawaii 49

Davida Malo 53

Lydia Liliuokalani 56

Charles Edward King 58

Mary Kawena Pukui 60

Pablo Manlapit 62

Carlos Bulosan 64

D.T. Suzuki 68

Philip Vera Cruz 70

Chiura Obata 73

Inmates in America's
Detention Camps 77

A Case Against the Internment
of Japanese Americans 85

The 442nd
Combat Regiment 89

Sessue (Kintaro) Hayakawa 92

Yoshiko Uchida 96

Isamu Noguchi 100

James Wong Howe 104

Dalip Singh Saund 107

Younghill Kang 109

Anna May Wong 111

Samuel Ichiye Hayakawa 114

Hiram Fong 117

Sirdar Jagjit Singh 120

Toshio Mori 122

Chang-Ho Ahn 124

Philip Ahn 124

Dong Kingman 127

Bienvenido Nuqui Santos 130

Chien Shiung Wu 132

Minoru Yamasaki 135

Masayuki Matsunaga 138

I. M. Pei 140

An Wang 144

Sammy Lee 148

Jade Snow Wong 150

Daniel K. Inouye 153

Anna Chennault 156

Tsung Dao Lee 158

Chen Ning Yang 158

Gerard Tsai, Jr. 161

Patsy Takemoto Mink 163

K. W. Lee 165

Toshiko Akiyoshi 168

Jose Aruego 170

Seiji Ozawa 173

Zubin Mehta 176

Allen Say 178

Bette Bao Lord 180

Maxine Hong Kingston 183

Fred & Dorothy Cordova 186

Bruce Lee 188

Dith Pran 191

Luoth Yin 196

Korean American
  Grocery and Convenience
  Store Business 199

Nam June Paik 201

Wendy Lee Gramm 204

Ellison S. Onizuka 206

Connie Chung 209

Lawrence Yep 211

June Kuramoto 213

Wayne Wang 215

Amy Tan 217

Myung-Whun Chung 219

Yo-Yo Ma 222

David Henry Hwang 224

Vietnamese Boat People 227

The Hmong: Refugees from Laos 233

Maya Ying Lin 236

Eugene H. Trinh 239

Greg Louganis 241

Andy Leonard 244

Midori 247

Michael Chang 250

Kristi Yamaguchi 252

Notes 254

Further Reading 255

Index 262

Acknowledgments 269

About the Author and Illustrator 270

Preface

The Chinese have been painting exquisite images on silk for more than a thousand years. Among the most enduring subjects to grace the fine, delicate fabrics of Chinese silk is the dragon. The mysterious, benevolent beast represents the powerful forces of the universe and warns humans against disrupting a fragile harmony.

On the oldest silk canvases, the dragon stands alone, surrounded only by the open space of the background fabric. As Chinese painting became a more sophisticated art form, however, dragons were combined with other images and the whole seemed to move in a common rhythm. The dragon, no longer lost in silken space, became a part of the broader world of the artwork.

In writing a book that attempts to group many different people under the title "Asian Pacific Americans," there is always the risk that the biographies will seem — just like the images of early Chinese paintings — juxtaposed on, but not integrated into, a shared background. My hope is that the space, both literal and figurative, between the biographies in this book will link, rather than isolate, the subjects. And then, as on an artful canvas, the images will find a common cadence.

Susan Sinnott

A Note about the Art

On the cover of the book *Extraordinary Asian Pacific Americans* is a delicately designed dragon drawn on top of an intricate background pattern. It is a composite of different elements depicted in dragons found in the ancient art of Japan, China, Korea, India, Indonesia, and Southeast Asia. Floating in a ghosted circle confined within a square, the dominant dragon represents a presence in two very diverse cultures (the East and the West) that have two remarkably different ways of viewing the world. The dragon appears "at home" in its flowery background, perhaps because it is a symbol of nature and of life itself. The background, which is from a silk dress sent by the designer's grandfather to her mother from southern China in 1949, was scanned into a computer and then made into film for the cover.

In Asian cultures, the dragon epitomizes strength and goodness. It is a divine animal that changes its appearance and personality at will, reducing itself to a tiny silk worm or swelling to a size that could fill the space of heaven and earth. Dragons vigilantly protect the mansions of the gods and wield great power over nature.

The book cover and the decorative borders and sketches found throughout this book were designed and illustrated by the designer on a computer. They resemble many of the symbols, characters, and elements of nature found in the art and intricate motifs of several Asian countries.

Asian Pacific American Immigration

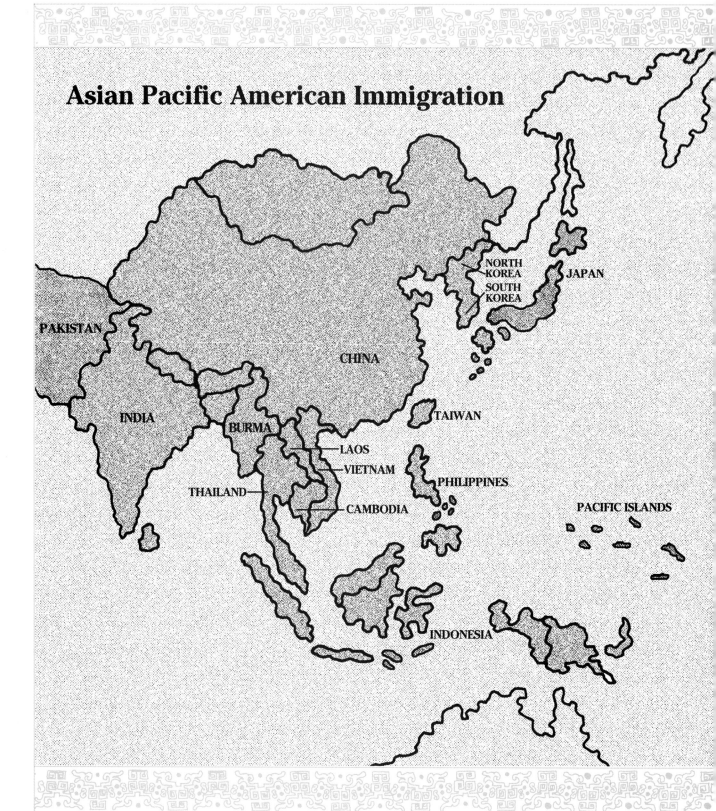

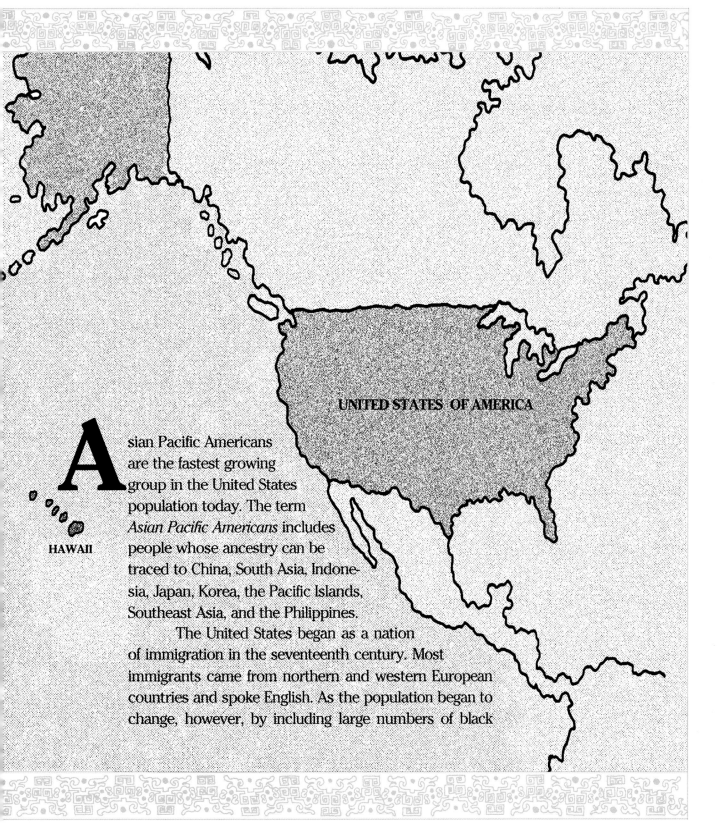

UNITED STATES OF AMERICA

HAWAII

Asian Pacific Americans are the fastest growing group in the United States population today. The term *Asian Pacific Americans* includes people whose ancestry can be traced to China, South Asia, Indonesia, Japan, Korea, the Pacific Islands, Southeast Asia, and the Philippines.

The United States began as a nation of immigration in the seventeenth century. Most immigrants came from northern and western European countries and spoke English. As the population began to change, however, by including large numbers of black slaves from Africa and other non-European, non-English-speaking groups, American founders felt it necessary to restrict eligibility for citizenship. In 1790 Congress passed a law restricting naturalization only to "free white persons." When the Fourteenth Amendment to the U. S. Constitution was adopted in 1868, granting citizenship to all persons born in the United States, the existing naturalization law was modified to include "aliens of African nativity and persons of African descent." Still Congress chose not to extend naturalization rights to Asians, thus making them the only racial group barred from naturalization. Because the Fourteenth Amendment granted citizenship to all persons born in the United States, American-born children of Asian immigrants automatically became citizens. (Only in 1947 were Filipinos and Asian Indians granted eligibility for naturalization. Not until 1952 was naturalization eligibility extended to all races.)

Despite discriminatory immigration and naturalization laws, immigrants came to the United States from several Asian countries. The first Asians to arrive in large numbers were Chinese. Some time during the 1840s they began arriving in Hawaii to work on sugarcane plantations. During the 1850s they emigrated to the West Coast of the United States to work in gold mines and later to help build the transcontinental railroad connecting the East and West Coasts. In the late nineteenth and early twentieth centuries waves of Japanese, Filipinos, Koreans, and Asian Indians arrived.

Unlike European immigrants, who were allowed to become citizens of the United States and encouraged to take part in all aspects of American life, Asian immigrants were denied citizenship and kept out of the main-stream. In addition, most West Coast states had what were called *alien land laws* which made it illegal for aliens who could not become citizens to own land. Prejudice against Asians became so strong that in 1882 Congress passed the first of the Chinese Exclusion Acts preventing the importation of Chinese laborers. In 1907 the same restrictions were applied to Japanese laborers. Later, the Immigration Act of 1917 enacted a literacy test and

A Chinese woman reading her Bible

banned immigration from all countries in the Asia-Pacific Triangle except for the Philippines (a U. S. territory) and Japan. Then in 1924 all Asian immigration was cut off. The only group of would-be Asian Americans not restricted were those from the Philippines, although they could not become American citizens.

It was not until after World War II that these laws were revised. In 1945 the War Brides Act made it legal for the wives and children of U. S. servicemen to enter the country and become citizens. Congress passed several special acts admitting refugees. It was not until 1952 that the bars to naturalization of Asians were taken down. But the 1952 Immigration and Naturalization Act retained strong restrictions on immigration from the Asia-Pacific Triangle. It also based immigration on a national origins quota system. That is, if people from a certain country made up ten percent of the U. S. population, then up to ten percent of the annual total for immigration could come from that country. Clearly, since immigration from Asia had been cut off for nearly twenty years and there were not that many Asian Americans to begin with, this placed further restrictions on Asians who wanted to come to the United States.

The 1965 amendments to the Immigration and Naturalization Act repealed the national origins provision and set an annual equal limit of twenty thousand for every country in the Eastern Hemisphere. But more important, there was a new preference system that gave first choice to immigrants having close family ties in the United States or to those having special skills. This change in immigration laws produced the second major wave of Asian immigration into the United States. This time, however, the groups were heavily Filipino, Korean, Chinese, and Southeast Asian.

After South Vietnam and Cambodia fell to Communist forces in 1975 and U. S. troops withdrew, large numbers of refugees asked for admission into the United States. (Refugees, unlike immigrants, do not leave their homeland willingly. War, famine, or other catastrophies force them out.)

The Immigration Reform and Control Act of 1986 made family relationships and skills — not national origin — the basis for allowing immigrants into the United States. As a result, the kinds of immigrants coming to America changed completely.

Ever since the change in immigration laws allowing more Asian Pacific immigrants and refugees into the United States, there has been an extraordinary growth rate. According to a 1990 census, Asian Pacific Americans made up 2.9 percent of the American population. This was a 95 percent increase from the 1980 census. It is expected that the Asian Pacific population in the year 2020 will be around 19 million, nearly a 150 percent increase over the 7 million in 1990.

As this growth continues, adjustments will have to be made and new policies considered not only in the Asian Pacific American community, but also in the nation as a whole — policies that will incorporate more Asian Pacific Americans into the political and economic fabric of American life and enable them to contribute successfully in building a strong, multicultural democracy.

Tan The Ha (right) and his brother-in-law take a break from their thirteen-hour work day outside their Saigon Market in Arlington, Virginia.

Panning for gold in California

Travelers to Gold Mountain

In the Chinese villages of Canton province, news of the comings and goings of trading ships at the nearby port of Hong Kong was eagerly awaited. As soon as a clipper ship docked, crowds gathered to hear the tales of its well-traveled crew. The lands across the sea, it seemed, were full of wondrous treasures. When, in 1848, word spread that gold had been discovered in faraway California, the lure of *Gum Saan* — Gold Mountain — was too strong to ignore.

To be sure, the risks of leaving China were great. In emigration, as in other matters, the policies of China's imperial government were harsh. Young men were needed for the Emperor's army and for public works projects, and so anyone caught leaving their homes and families to work abroad would certainly face the executioner's axe.

And, as if the death penalty weren't enough, the would-be emigrant also had to go against the teachings of Confucius that guided the Chinese in all matters of daily life. Confucius taught that children must always devote themselves to their parents and ancestors. Leaving one's family and ancestral home, therefore, was a grave offense against Chinese tradition.

What then would make a young Chinese man risk everything to sail for the Gold Mountain? Simply, that he had everything to gain — even life itself. In the mid-nineteenth century, Canton was a rocky, barren province and its farmers could only grow enough food to feed its large population for four months out of the year. Because there was no industry, the only way for the Cantonese to assure their own survival was to send at least one male family member abroad.

Not surprisingly then, more and more men sought passage to America. Even after California's generous gold veins gave out, thousands clamored for the opportunity to work across the ocean. The rewards were so great that families did everything possible to get one of their relatives onto a ship. By 1851 25,000 Chinese "travelers" were in California.

What were the experiences of these thousands of young men? In her book *Mountain of Gold*, Betty Lee Sung tells the story of a young Chinese man named Fatt Hing Chin, whose story is typical of other early emigrants to the United States. Here is a summary.

Fatt Hing was nineteen. While earning a living peddling fish along the wharves, he heard stories about Gold Mountain. News of this faraway place had become almost as valuable to local people as the goods bought and sold on the docks, and Fatt Hing made up his mind to seek his fortune there. He knew of the dangers. Many, he'd heard, had been arrested boarding ships and taken off to certain deaths. But he'd heard, too, that certain soldiers could be bribed, and he took the time to find out which ones. Then, with great difficulty, he convinced his worried parents to sell a water buffalo and some family jewelry in order to pay the high price of smuggling him onto a Spanish ship bound for San Francisco.

The passage took three months. The ship's hold was full of other young men, who, like Fatt Hing, were illegal stowaways. For the first time in Fatt Hing's life, he was surrounded by strangers. Many became sick during the long voyage and some died. All were miserable. By the time the hills of San Francisco came into view, many of the Chinese wondered if, in fact, they would ever see a speck of gold. Many believed they had been sold into slavery and would never see China again.

When the ship finally docked though, the stowaways were relieved to see several Chinese men waiting for them on land. These men greeted the new arrivals and took them to the headquarters of the Six Companies in San Francisco's Chinatown. There the men were fed and told what to expect in America. The most important thing they learned was to look out for each other within the new and often hostile environment.

"... One valuable lesson we have learned and which you will soon appreciate,' the chairman of the Six Companies told Fatt Hing and the others, '... is that we must stick together and help one another, even though we are not kin. That is why we have formed this organization called the Six Companies, representing the six districts which most of us come from. ..."[1]

Mining was backbreaking work and had little return for most Asian laborers.

The chairman then told the arrivals how to get along with the white miners, many of whom showed vicious anti-Chinese sentiment. "Be patient and maintain your dignity," the chairman told them, even when prejudicial treatment manifests itself in discriminatory laws, harrassment, and violence.

Following the chairman's advice, workers were given mining tools and told where and how to start. Within days of their arrival in California, the men headed for the hills. They worked furiously to loosen the earth from

Miners pause from their work to be photographed.

the mountainsides and wash out the fine gold particles. Unlike other miners, however, who had the advantage of working new claims, Chinese miners were allowed to work only leftover claims.

In spite of the prejudice and discrimination, Fatt Hing, like other courageous Chinese miners, was somehow able to rise above the unfair conditions. Unfortunately, he paid a heavy price in personal suffering for his small portion of gold dust, which he quickly sent back to his family in China. Not wanting his family to know about the ill-treatment he and others were receiving in America, Fatt Hing only wrote about the good things. Once he scribbled a single message inside one of the packets he sent home: "Truly these are mountains of gold!"

When profits in gold mining began to decrease in the mid-1860s, Chinese laborers started leaving the gold fields for jobs in railroad construction, fieldwork, and limited employment opportunities in San Francisco. Prejudice and discrimination, however, followed close behind.

Using only picks and shovels, black powder and hand drills, Chinese laborers built the Central Pacific Railroad through the Sierra Nevada of California.

Chinese Railroad Workers

1860s

Years of bickering preceded the decision in 1862 to build a transcontinental railroad across the United States. With the Civil War threatening to pull the nation apart, Congress quickly passed the Pacific Railroad Act, which was then signed into law by President Abraham Lincoln. The law gave financial backing to two companies — the Central Pacific and Union Pacific — to lay the track that would link the East Coast to the West.

Among the problems encountered by the Big Four railroad tycoons — Charles Crocker, Leland Stanford, Collis P. Huntington, and Mark Hopkins — was where to find workers for such a huge project. Charles Crocker, who was head of construction for the Central Pacific, decided to try Chinese labor. He had heard that, despite being physically small, the Chinese worked hard and long for very low wages. Crocker believed that they, unlike the Union Pacific's mostly Irish crews, would not risk striking to gain better wages or working conditions.

With this in mind, Crocker recruited fifty Chinese workers and sent them, picks in hand, to the Central Pacific work site. From the first day they performed beyond anyone's expectations, working without complaint for fourteen hours. Impressed by their conduct, Crocker immediately began recruiting Chinese laborers from Chinatown, and later directly from China. By 1869 nearly 15,000 Chinese workers were employed by the Central Pacific. Competition was fierce between the Union Pacific, which was working its way west through Nebraska and Wyoming, and the Central Pacific, which was making its way eastward through the Sierra Nevadas. Because the U. S. government was paying the companies for the miles of track laid, construction bosses pushed their workers hard.

There was never any question who had the more difficult task. The Central Pacific had to pick its way by hand through the huge granite walls of the Sierra Nevada that rose steeply to heights of 7,000 feet (2,134 m). The Union Pacific crews, on the other hand, made their way through the more gradual rise of the Black Hills. Many wondered if any humans could complete the task facing the Union Pacific's Chinese workers — first the steep mountain faces, then the bitter cold, the blinding snows, and the avalanches during one of the coldest winters in western history. At one point during the winter of 1865–66, almost 5,000 men were put to work just clearing snow. They dug tunnels beneath the huge drifts and for months traveled like moles from living quarters to work, scarcely seeing above the snow's surface.

As the heroic work of the Chinese became known, the Irish workers of the Union Pacific began to openly express their jealousy. The leaders of each railroad used this spirited competition to get even more work from their men. Once, when the Central Pacific laid down six miles (9.7 km) of track, word was quickly sent to the Union Pacific bosses. The next day, the proud Irish answered back with seven miles (11.3 km). Near the finish point, Charles Crocker wagered $10,000 that his Chinese workers could lay ten miles (16.1 km) of track in one day. Mr. Durant, president of the Union Pacific, accepted the bet. The Chinese completed the ten miles and added a half mile for good measure!

These Chinese pioneers, who laid 689 miles (1,109 km) of railroad track, contributed greatly to opening up the West to commerce and settlement. Yet, when the last spike — the Golden Spike — was driven into the railroad ties on May 10, 1869 at Promontory, Utah, linking the Central Pacific and Union Pacific railroads, no Asian workers were included in the historical photograph. This omission foretold worse things ahead as 25,000 railroad workers poured into California looking for new jobs.

By 1870 unemployment in California was dangerously high. Political leaders, eager to find a scapegoat for the state's economic problems, blamed the hard-working Chinese. And the Chinese, who stood out in their traditional dress and long queues, or pigtails, were easy targets. Shortly after being praised for their extraordinary work on the railroad, the Chinese were openly scorned and even attacked by disgruntled workers. As the nineteenth century came to a close, the Chinese of California found themselves in an even more uncertain situation than when they had first arrived to work on the railroad.

Although Chinese laborers were responsible for building the western portion of the Transcontinental Railroad, they are noticeably absent from the historic photograph taken on May 10, 1869, in Promontory, Utah.

Yung Wing
Educator, Diplomat
1828–1912

Yung Wing spent his life straddling two very different cultures. One foot was placed in the country of his birth and ancestry, China; the other was firmly fixed in his adopted homeland, the United States. He felt close to both yet secure in neither.

Yung Wing was born in 1828 in the village of Nam Ping near the former Portuguese trading colony of Macao. Because Macao was a bustling port, with clipper ships arriving often from all over the world, Yung Wing — unlike many other Chinese of his day — was familiar with the West. His parents, strongly influenced by the success of the local shipping trade, decided that their son's measure of success in life would depend on his obtaining a Western-style education.

Their wish was granted when, with the financial help of a Chinese minister who had been educated at Yale University in the United States, Yung and two other Chinese boys were selected to attend a preparatory school in the United States. In April 1847, Yung Wing arrived in Massachusetts and enrolled at Monson Academy. He adjusted well to his new life and, after graduating in 1850, wanted nothing more than to stay in the United States. There were two problems, however. First, he had promised his parents that he would return to China after two years, which he had already extended to three. Second, how could he afford the high cost of continuing his studies?

Fortunately for Yung, two sponsors came forward to fund his education. After many pleading letters exchanged with family members, Yung's parents agreed that it was in their son's best interests to stay in America. In 1850 Yung Wing became both a Yale freshman and the first Chinese ever to enroll at an American college.

Immediately, Wing rose to the academic challenges of Yale. "I never was subject to such excitement," he wrote one of his sponsors those first few months. "I enjoy its influence very much."

During Yung Wing's years at Yale, he developed an affinity for the United States. He appreciated its way of life and became a naturalized citizen in 1853. But because he was confused about the direction his life should take, he decided to return to China after graduation.

In China Wing tried to convince the Imperial Government of the importance of sending Chinese boys to school in the United States. He firmly believed that for China to be able to enter the modern world, its people would need technological training available only abroad. Wing hoped he could play an active role in such an educational venture in the future.

After working several years as a silk and tea importer, Wing was asked by the Imperial Chinese Government to be their trade negotiator with the United States. Before leaving for Washington, D.C., he again proposed the idea of an American education to the government in Beijing. To his surprise, the response was favorable. Now even normally close-minded government officials were beginning to see the value of instructing young men in the uses of European and American technology. Acceptance turned to action in 1872 when thirty Chinese boys were sent to Hartford, Connecticut, to study. Thirty new students would follow each year of the program.

In America Yung Wing's ties to China became increasingly weaker while his bonds to the United States became increasingly stronger. In 1875 he married an American woman, Mary Kellogg. The same year, China set up its first permanent mission in the United States and named Yung Wing associate minister — second in command after the ambassador. Wing's fluent English made him popular with American officials and he used his influence to improve the situation of Chinese workers in the United States. He was outraged by the prejudicial treatment they received and didn't hesitate to say so.

Despite Wing's sincere efforts, the Chinese education mission lasted less than ten years. Officials of the Imperial Government, believing Wing was encouraging students to adopt an alien way of life while they were being trained in technology, called him back to China in 1881 to take stock of his government duties. He stayed one year, returning as soon as he heard of his wife's grave illness. After Mary died in 1886, Wing devoted himself to raising his two sons, writing, and lecturing.

Photograph taken in the 1870s of Yung Wing (third from left) and students from the Chinese Educational Mission

In 1898, almost fifty years after becoming a citizen of the United States, Wing received a telegram from the U. S. State Department telling him that his citizenship had been revoked. The reason given was that a change in the naturalization law had made his earlier application invalid. Wing begged friends to help him reverse the decision, but no amount of influence changed the government's mind.

Yung Wing left the United States and settled for a while in Hong Kong. In 1902 he returned to the United States, successfully slipping past immigration authorities. He lived out his life in Hartford, Conneticut, near his sons and their families. While back in the States, Wing was visited often by American and Chinese friends and consulted on questions of American-Chinese relations. In 1909 his autobiography, *My Life in China and in America,* was published. It was the first English-language autobiography by an Asian American.

A Manchu lady and Chinese woman

Prisoners of Angel Island

By 1900 stories reaching China of the abundant riches in California were more fable than fact. Anti-Asian feelings among whites in America had made life very difficult for the Chinese. The Chinese Exclusion Act of 1882, which had singled out one ethnic group for discrimination, was never challenged. In fact, by the turn of the century, amendments to the law made it even harsher than originally intended.

The Exclusion Law attempted to stop all Chinese laborers or their families from entering the U. S. The only immigrants welcome from China were officials, teachers, some students, and tourists. This left Chinese workers in America, almost all men, in a desperate situation. Their families in China depended on the money that was sent to them from America. Without income from abroad, many would starve because southern China could not support its large population. But enforcement of the Exclusion Law meant that there was no hope families could reunite in the States.

Many of the young men who had left their homes for America shortly after marrying, expected their separation would be brief. Believing this, many wives happily saw their husbands off. As one popular Chinese rhyme suggested:

If you have a daughter,
marry her quickly
to a traveler to Gold Mountain.
For when he gets off the boat,
he will bring hundreds of
pieces of silver.[2]

Chinese from the better class in Canton, China

Indeed, sometimes the silver did arrive, and occasionally the husbands. In America Chinatowns became full of homeless, lonely men, and in China "widows" raised fatherless children. The strong ties that traditionally bound Chinese families were being broken.

Some Chinese men, desperate to be reunited with their families, looked for any possible loophole in the immigration law. Some tried to convince authorities that they were not common laborers at all but merchants. Others produced papers claiming they were native born. Few of these schemes succeeded.

Help finally came to Chinese laborers in an unexpected form. On April 18, 1906, as Chinatown residents recalled, the earth dragon split the ground beneath the city of San Francisco. Buildings toppled and burst into flames. Nearly 28,000 structures were destroyed by a great earthquake — including the city's municipal buildings, where records of births, deaths, and marriages were stored. Now all of a sudden, there was no way to verify the most basic facts of someone's life.

Many residents of Chinatown took advantage of this opportunity to claim they had been born in San Francisco, and according to U. S. law, their children, even if they were born in a foreign country, were automatically U. S. citizens. As proof of citizenship, the residents forged their own birth certificates and sent money to their families to come to America.

Soon, however, immigration authorities caught on to this tactic and devised ways to make entry difficult. They used the law, which required immigrants to undergo a period of detainment at either Ellis Island in New York or Angel Island in California, to interrogate Chinese families and force many of them to return to China. Of all Chinese who were detained at Angel Island, ten percent were sent back to China.

All immigrants coming through Angel Island had to pass an examination to prove their American identity. They were not released until they had convinced authorities that their identity papers were legitimate. Often, the questioning, which was designed to confuse and trick immigrants, went on for hours. Usually it had nothing to do with whether the person had a right to enter the United States or not. For example, someone might be asked small details about his or her life in China: "How many chickens did your grandfather own? Where was the village pond? What did your mother's water jug look like?" Answers were checked against those of relatives and any differences were taken as proof of fraud.

Women with children wait to be interrogated at Angel Island immigration station .

San Francisco's Angel Island was known for its unsanitary conditions and unfair interrogation procedures. The building where immigrants were detained was a two-story shed that extended out over the water, connecting the wharf by a narrow stairway. The small, smelly rooms were bare and resembled cages in a zoo. Minimal amounts of food were served — usually thrown — on the floor. Some Chinese waited in these squalid conditions for up to four months before authorities called them in for questioning.

Ironically, because of the interrogations, many who had the legal right to enter the United States were often denied it. They simply weren't aware that they would be asked pointless, rambling questions and, as a result, couldn't adequately prepare. In time, the immigration law and the way immigrants were processed through Angel Island became so twisted that authorities could not tell who should and shouldn't enter the country. It wasn't until 1943 that the Chinese Exclusion Act was repealed.

San Francisco's Chinatown

Chinese Benevolent Associations and Tongs

In New York they're called the Chinese Consolidated Benevolent Associations; in San Francisco, the Chinese Six Companies, after the six regions from which most Chinese emigrated; in Honolulu, the United Chinese Society. Their purpose is the same: to offer protection, security, and aid to recent arrivals from China. For one hundred and fifty years, these associations have saved many Chinese from having to face prejudice and discrimination. However, they also have isolated many Chinese and kept them out of the prosperous mainstream of American life.

As the population of Chinese laborers grew in the United States and became concentrated in cities like San Francisco, New York, and Chicago, racial discrimination and violence directed against them intensified. To protect themselves from the violence and create an environment of security and social and economic support, the Chinese built self-sufficient communities called Chinatowns. The Chinatown in San Francisco was the largest. During the 1850s, it was a bustling business community of general merchandise stores, restaurants, boarding houses, butcher shops, and tailor shops. Nine years later, it had grown six blocks long. The second largest Chinatown is in New York City.

Organizations abounded in Chinatowns. The first level of organization was the family association or clan groups, which included all Chinese bearing the same last name. In China all Chens and Lees and Hongs are assumed to be related, no matter how slight the blood ties. And since there are only 438 last names for a billion or so people worldwide, the associations can be huge. Because many people who shared last names tended to settle in the same part of the United States — for example, the Lees in

Washington, D.C., and the Moys in Chicago — family associations became very powerful. Their purpose was to provide financial assistance, offer temporary housing, and maintain the social centers.

The second level of organization was the regional, or district association. It was identified by language and was made up of the districts or regions from which Chinese had originated. These were the largest associations and the ones having the most control over every aspect of Chinatown society. They were responsible for welcoming new arrivals and for providing housing and finding employment for them. District associations helped settle interdistrict conflicts and provided educational and health services to the community. They founded newspapers and radio stations and set rules for competition among Chinese institutions. Their protests against anti-Chinese activities and discriminatory laws lead the way to more just government legislation.

Today district associations are still active in Chinatowns. In New York City, for example, forty organizations are represented at monthly meetings of the benevolent association. The president, elected by delegates for a two-year term, is one of the most powerful leaders in the community. He presides at public functions, organizes celebrations, and settles arguments.

District associations have always held tight control over residents and businesses in Chinatowns. In fact, those wishing to open up businesses must have their approval. Without association support, small business owners could find themselves without workers or needed capital. Powerful association leaders could block rental agreements within a Chinatown and a would-be store owner could find himself or herself without a storefront.

This strict control has kept American government officials out of the lives of average Chinatown residents, but in turn has denied them access to the "real" America. As a result, the Chinese in Chinatowns have remained strangers to the American way of life far longer than most emigrants. Also, it has encouraged the development of *tongs* (secret societies) among those in the Chinese community who refused to be controlled by the established associations. Over time, the *tongs*, which were led by criminals who controlled gambling houses and drug and prostitution rings, became a feared and hated part of the Chinese underworld.

Police guarding the headquarters of a tong group in Washington, D.C.'s Chinatown in 1927, hoping to avert further fighting between rival factions

Today tongs and benevolent associations have lost their tight control over America's Chinese communities. Since 1949, many Chinese have arrived in the U. S. from parts of China other than the original six regions. Their educational and professional levels are much higher than earlier emigrés, enabling them to work in American society without the help of a benevolent association. In fact, the Chinese who have emigrated to the United States since the 1950s usually have had little to do with the nation's Chinatowns. They view them in much the same way as other Americans do — as interesting places where they can visit and shop or as historical sites where they can celebrate Chinese New Year, but not as a controlling influence in their lives. Future refugees, however, may change this.

Chinese participating in a small Idaho town parade in the early 1900s

Polly Bemis (Lalu Nathoy)
Idaho Pioneer
1853–1933

Nineteen-year-old Lalu Nathoy waited in the San Francisco customs shed for her turn to stand before the officer. She thought of the journey she had just completed from China in the hold of a cargo ship, of the weeks in the sweltering heat amid vomit and human waste, and of the terrible loneliness and fear that still overwhelmed her. Thoughts of her family in China and the unfortunate series of events that had brought her to America filled her memories.

Lalu Nathoy (later called Polly Bemis) was born in China in 1853 during a time of famine and political unrest. Her parents struggled desperately to harvest just enough food to survive and pay for the upkeep of their tiny farm. To help support the family, Lalu's parents thought of hiring her out to wealthy landowners as other families had done with their daughters. But they listened instead to Lalu's pleas to remain at home and work with her father in the fields.

Before Lalu could work in the fields, the binding that was wrapped tightly around her feet had to be removed. In China it was customary to wrap, or bind, girls feet tightly with cloth so that their feet would remain small and delicate. Unbinding Lalu's feet and letting her work like a man would bring shame and insults, besides jeopardizing her chances for marriage. Nevertheless, it was what she wanted. So for the next five years, Lalu worked hard in the fields, doing what no other young girl in her district had done. No matter how hard she and others worked, however, the famine continued. And with the famine came hundreds of marauding bandits, riding into villages to steal food and whatever else they could sell.

On the day they charged into the Nathoy's home, Lalu's life changed forever. When the bandits threatened to kill her family and destroy their home unless Lalu agreed to go with them, Lalu's father had no alternative but to sell her. Leaving two bags of soybeans, the bandits left with Lalu. She never saw or communicated with her family again. Eventually she was sold to a Shanghai brothel owner, who, in turn, offered her to a "special buyer" in America.

When the San Francisco customs officer was finally finished questioning Lalu, she was taken to a Chinatown marketplace. There she was auctioned to the highest bidder and put on a ship that sailed up the coast to Portland, Oregon. From there a Chinese man drove her along many miles of rugged trail to the makeshift mining town of Warrens, Idaho. In Warrens, Lalu was delivered to her new master, a Chinese saloon owner named Hong King. And it was there that she began answering to a new name, Polly.

Polly's old, miserly owner cheated and abused her. After awhile she devised plans for running away and even thought about how she could get rid of him. Freedom came to her, however, in an unexpected way. One day, after Hong King had lost everything he owned in a poker game to a fellow Warrens saloon owner named Charlie Bemis, he had to forfeit his right to ownership of Polly. For Polly, this meant that her luck had finally turned around.

Charlie Bemis was willing to allow Polly two things she had not felt for a long time: love and freedom. With these gifts and the money that she was now able to save, Polly opened a four-room boarding house in Warrens where she became one of its most trusted and respected citizens.

Townspeople talked often of Polly's rare power to make others happy and healthy. Her ability to nurse the sick became legendary. Once, when

Charlie had been shot in the head by a drunken customer and the local doctor gave him no chance of recovering, she nursed him back to health by applying Chinese herbal medicines.

Polly ran her popular boarding house until she married Charlie in her late forties. The two then headed into the Idaho wilderness, where they homesteaded 20 acres (8 hectares) of land along the Salmon River. After Charlie died in 1922, Polly lived in their rustic mountain cabin as long as she was able to manage on her own. When she died in Warrens in 1933, the whole town turned out to honor her.

Lalu Nathoy's struggle for survival and freedom in China, during her passage to America, and within the confines of early Idaho mining towns, is a lesson in the power of the human spirit and its ability to overcome the most devasting experiences and find happiness.

Polly in front of her rustic Idaho mountain cabin

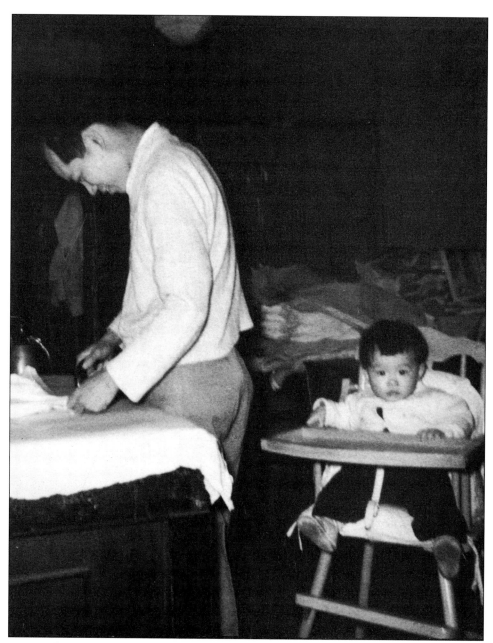

For many Chinese families, the laundry was a place where they both lived and worked.

The Chinese Laundry Business

"The neon sign of a Chinese hand laundry reminded Charles of the several shirts he had not yet picked up. . . . He entered the shop and saw the old man still hard at work behind the counter, ironing under a naked electric bulb, although it was already ten o'clock at night. . . .

'How many years have you been in the States?' Charles asked out of curiosity as he paid the man.

'Forty years,' the old man answered in Cantonese. No expression showed on his face.

'Do you have a family?'

'Big family. A woman, many sons and grandsons. All back home in Tangshan.' From underneath the counter he brought out a photograph and showed it to Charles. In the center sat a white-haired old woman, surrounded by some fifteen or twenty men, women, and children of various ages. The whole clan, with contented expressions on their faces, were the off-spring of this emaciated old man, who supported not only himself but all of them by his two shaking, bony hands. . . ."[3]

By the late nineteenth century the passage of anti-Chinese laws had already forced many Chinese workers out of most agricultural and manufacturing jobs. Competing with whites had become both difficult and humiliating, so the Chinese, in large numbers, began opening laundries. With just a washtub and an ironing board, one could open a business and earn a modest living.

By 1886 7,500 Chinese were engaged in the laundry business. Despite the fact that laundries were not common in China and most Chinese men considered washing "women's work," Chinese immigrants in the United States learned how to make the laundry business work for them. Laundries allowed the Chinese worker to be his or her own boss and to work within the Chinese community, thereby avoiding daily discrimination. Knowing how to speak English well was not a requirement for opening a store. Most launderers never needed to know more than a few English words to run a successful business.

As the Chinese left the large cities of California and headed east, they found they could open laundries almost anywhere. In large cities such as Denver, St. Louis, and Chicago, they could find low-rent quarters, put out a sign, and begin taking in laundry almost immediately. Because they provided pickup and delivery, the location and appearance of the store was unimportant. Many Chinese laundries were located in white neighborhoods where Chinese usually were not allowed to live. So launderers lived instead in the overcrowded ghettos of Chinatowns.

It's not surprising then that for at least half a century, the main occupation of the Chinese in the United States was washing and ironing. In 1920 there were four Chinese laundries for every Chinese restaurant, the other common business.

The money sent to China by laundrymen often allowed large extended families to live comfortably. Usually a family relied on a single person working long, lonely hours in the United States. Many never knew the hardships a Chinese worker had to endure in America. Laundry work was boring and lonely. The income provided for only a minimal standard of living. Because many immigrants had gone into debt to pay for their passage to America, a good deal of their income went toward the payment of their loans. A little was taken out for living expenses, and the rest was sent to their families in China who depended on it for their survival.

In time, many new arrivals saw laundry work as more of a prison sentence than a job. They worked day in and day out, but dreamed only of the day they could return to China. In the words of one young man interviewed about fifty years ago:

". . . People think I am a happy person. I am not. I worry very much. First, I don't like this kind of life. . . . To be a laundryman is to be just a slave. I work because I have to. . . . After you are at it for so many years, you have no more feeling but to stay on with it." [4]

Most of those who entered the laundry business stayed with it until far into the twentieth century. Today, new immigrants are opening dry cleaning stores, shoe repair stores, and other quick cashflow businesses that require a minimum of English and allow the whole family to work.

The Chinese laundry business was a family occupation.

Joe Shoong
Businessman, Philanthropist
1879–1961

Joe Shoong did what few other Chinese businessmen were able to do in California in 1905 — break the racial barriers of the business community and open a successful clothing store.

Breaking racial barriers and business stereotypes was no easy task. At a time when discriminatory practices of the white business community limited Asians to a few menial professions and generally kept businesses within the boundaries of the Chinese community, Shoong refused to be restricted by these practices. He took China Toggery, a small struggling women's clothing store, moved it from Vallejo, California, to San Francisco's Fillmore District, and set out to sell his goods as fast and as cheaply as possible. This daring business risk paid off. Business boomed after the earthquake of 1906, and by 1921 his one store had become a chain.

Joe's parents had been among San Francisco's earliest Chinese settlers, having arrived during the 1850s. As a second generation Chinese and San Franciscan, Joe felt he understood the city's buying public, both Chinese and otherwise. He seemed to know what the consumers of the city wanted and gave it to them at the best possible price.

By 1921 Shoong's single store had become a chain called the China-Toggery-Shoong Company. Seven years later, the number of stores increased to sixteen and the name was changed to National Dollar Stores. The new name advertised the fact that the first stores sold no merchandise for more than a dollar. Low prices attracted attention, and the stores were very popular and always crowded. As one customer remembered, "the clerks would open boxes of sheets or towels and sell each one for just over cost."

Although all National Dollar Stores were owned and operated by Chinese, they appealed to the average California shopper. Customer lines formed quickly and all the goods went very fast. Business prospered until 1937 when a workers' strike threatened to close the Dollar Stores.

That year Chinese garment workers who made clothing for the Dollar Stores had organized a union to get better pay and working conditions. They called themselves the Chinese Ladies Garment Workers. Assisted by the AFL-CIO, the most powerful labor union in America, the Chinese Ladies Garment Workers staged a strike against the Dollar Stores garment factory. The strike lasted thirteen weeks, the longest in Chinatown history. Although the workers fought valiantly for their rights, they ultimately lost their battle when Joe Shoong closed the garment factory rather than give in to their demands.

Once Joe Shoong, the man *Time* magazine called "the richest, best-known Chinese businessman in the U. S." had become a millionaire, he was generous with his money. He gave large donations to the Chinese Hospital in San Francisco and to the Oakland Chinese Community Center. Scholarships for Chinese students to the University of California and other schools were also given in his name.

At the time of Joe Shoong's death on April 16, 1961, the National Dollar Store empire extended into seven western states and was worth twelve million dollars. Joe Shoong was listed as the second wealthiest man in California. But his success, which some critics called "ruthlessness," came at a price. Although he may have achieved what few Chinese businessmen were able to at the time, Joe Shoong made his fortune on the backs of poorly paid Chinese laborers — a tragedy some would never forgive.

A Japanese woman harvesting sugarcane in Hawaii

Raising Sugarcane in Hawaii

In 1877 the *Hawaiian Gazette* proclaimed, "Sugar is . . . King!" and everyone on the islands agreed. Native Hawaiian workers had made sugar production Hawaii's main industry. To ensure that sugar's reign would be a long one, plantation owners began recruiting cheap labor. The call went out to all able-bodied Asians to come to work on the islands, which were going to become a territory of the United States in 1900. Chinese workers came first, followed by Japanese, Koreans, and finally Filipinos. By the 1920s, more than 300,000 had signed on and settled down on one of the huge Hawaiian sugar plantations.

The conditions of emigration varied. The Japanese and Koreans tried to maintain family units while most Chinese and Filipino men had come alone. By the time the Filipinos arrived, the islands were fast approaching U. S. statehood (with annexation had come U. S. citizenship), and the Philippine Islands were well on their way to independence.

For the new arrivals who had time to look around, Hawaii seemed like a dreamland. The climate was close to perfect, the soil was rich, and the lush, green mountains seemed to hang from the clouds. Generally, however, most new workers were hustled off the ship and onto the plantations as quickly as possible. Once settled into their little shacks, the newcomers experienced the harsh realities that existed there. Those who had brought families soon learned that the rule of the plantation owner and his *luna*, or foreman, would dominate their lives.

The lunas and the police strode through the camps making sure all were ready for work. One Korean woman remembered the time her family didn't hear the work whistle and overslept: "Suddenly the door swung open and a big burly luna burst in, screaming and cursing, 'Get up, get to work.'

The luna ran around the room, ripping off the covers, not caring whether my family was dressed or not."

Field workers were grouped into gangs of twenty to thirty. Each worker was given a *bango*, which was a small, brass disc that had an identification number stamped on it, to wear around his or her neck. Thereafter, they would be called by their numbers rather than their names.

Workers laying a railroad track in a Hawaiian cane field

Workers were "treated no better than cows or horses," one laborer recalled. They operated like machines as lunas on horseback swung whips to keep the process moving. Plantation owners treated them like children, threatening them if they misbehaved. They were expected to be orderly, clean, and prompt, and would likely be fined or even whipped if they disobeyed the long list of regulations.

There was always plenty of work for everyone. When the cane was ripe, lines of men were led out to the fields to harvest the crop. They worked very fast, swinging their machetes back and forth through the forest of twelve-foot-high (3.7 m) sugarcane. When all the cane was cut, the workers tied the stalks into bundles and loaded them onto train cars. The train would then pull the cane to the mill. Inside the mill, machines crushed the cane and boiled its juices into molasses and sugar. The loud roar of the machines and the heat from the huge vats left workers confused and exhausted. "It was so hot with steam in the mill," one Japanese worker remembered, "that I became like *pupule* [crazy]."

To escape the harsh treatment imposed upon them, many workers, after awhile, disregarded their labor contracts and ran away. Others held out until their contracts expired and then moved on to what they thought would be better opportunities in Washington and California. The sugar owners tried hard to keep workers from leaving or from organizing and staging protests and strikes to improve the quality of their lives. But in 1900 alone, twenty strikes occurred.

Tension between workers and owners increased. In 1903 one luna hit a worker and was immediately set upon by a gang of Chinese men. In 1904 two hundred Korean laborers rioted when a plantation doctor kicked a patient in the stomach. In 1906 and 1909, Japanese laborers went on strike demanding higher wages and equal pay for equal work. After years of labor unrest on the sugar plantations, conditions began to improve. As workers' organizations and Filipino labor unions gradually developed, plantation owners were forced to change their work ethics. Then, too, second-generation Asians, who were educated in Hawaii's schools, would simply not work under the same conditions as their parents had. They demanded a better life.

Over the years, as life improved, Asian workers began to feel there was a place for them in Hawaii. They planted gardens and turned work camps into homes. The various ethnic groups, once alienated from each other, began communicating among themselves, eventually creating a pidgin English that developed into a common language. Groups built their own churches and temples and began to worship as they pleased. They freely practiced their native customs and traditions without suffering the prejudice and isolation that was becoming common on the U. S. mainland.

In time, these hard-working Asian immigrants became proud of their adopted homeland. Through their suffering and struggle, they had woven themselves and their cultures into the very fabric of Hawaii. Having transformed their adopted land into a society of rich diversity, many could proudly say, "Lucky come Hawaii."

Davida Malo
Author, Translator
1795–1853

Long before the arrival of the explorer Captain Cook at the Hawaiian Islands in 1778, and the European traders and American missionaries who followed him, there was a well-established culture on the islands. That we know anything about this remarkable time is due primarily to the research and writing of Davida Malo. The publication of his controversial book, *Ka Moolelo Hawaii (Hawaiian Antiquities)*, has furthered our understanding of native Hawaiian culture in prehistoric times.

Davida Malo was born on February 18, 1795, in the area of North Kona on the island of Hawaii. Both his parents were members of the court of King Kamehameha I, where Davida spent most of his youth. While in the courts of the high chief Kuakini, Davida learned about the traditional life and lore of Hawaiian chief society. During this time it is very probable that he also met American missionaries in the courts and received some Christian instruction.

Davida's parents encouraged his inquisitiveness and supported his eagerness to learn. Before long he became one of the most appealing youths of his time. While still in his teens, he married A'alaioa, the daughter of the King of Maui. She was much older than he, but it was customary for bright young men to improve their lives by marrying royalty. When A'alaioa died, sometime before 1822, Malo moved to Lahaina, Maui.

At Lahaina, Malo met Reverend William Richards, a Christian missionary. Under his guidance, Malo studied English and religion and was baptized in 1828. During this time, he and Richards worked on a translation of the Bible, which would later have a great influence on religious life in Hawaii. Malo also began keeping a record of Hawaiian geneologies (accounts of families from earliest times).

Malo began his formal education at Lahainaluna Seminary (high school) in 1831, when he was thirty-eight years old. But because he already had a background in western educational instruction from his days in the courts of Kuakini, he was more like a school master than a student at Lahainaluna. As one of Hawaii's first native-born Christians, he felt obligated to be a model for others at the school.

Malo's first literary work, a small religious tract, was published in 1837. After selling two thousand copies, the popular piece was reprinted in 1861 and 1865. His other writings offered advice in dealing with foreigners and warned Hawaiian leaders to improve communication among themselves or risk losing everything — including their uniquely Hawaiian way of life. He wrote, "The ships of the foreigners have come and smart people have arrived from the large nations. . . . They will eat us up, such has always been the case with large nations, the small ones have been gobbled up."

In between writing, Davida Malo turned his attention to growing sugarcane and producing molasses. A well-respected businessman, he was appointed General School Agent for the island of Maui in 1841, then Superintendent of Schools for the Kingdom, and finally elected as representative from Maui to the first House of Representatives of the Kingdom. The following year, he served as a member of the executive committee of the Temperance Society of Lahaina, and in 1844 was licensed to preach by the Hawaiian Association of American Ministers.

After the death of his second wife, Pahia Malo, in 1845, Malo married a third time. Although marriage to Lepeka (Rebecca) Malo caused him considerable grief, she gave him his only child, a daughter whom he named A'alaioa after his first wife.

By 1850 Davida Malo was so distraught by both his marital problems and a sense that Hawaiians were losing Hawaii that his health began to fail. Shortly after becoming an ordained minister, he remained in bed, refusing to eat or drink much. He died at Kalepolepo, Maui, three years later.

In 1903, fifty years after Davida Malo's death, all the volumes of *Hawaiian Antiquities* were translated. With its publication, the full breadth of Malo's intellect and influence were finally realized.

Lydia Liliuokalani
Musician, Queen
1838–1917

In the 1890s, Americans, who were called "mainlanders" on the Hawaiian Islands, believed that Queen Liliuokalani should reign but not rule. The Queen, however, who resented their control, was determined not to let that happen.

Born in Hawaii in 1838, Lydia Liliuokalani was a descendant of the prominent chiefs of the Big Island of Hawaii and sister of King David Kalakaua, whose death in 1891 brought her to power. Liliuokalani believed strongly that native Hawaiians should rule the islands. However, their dependence on foreign businesses and economic ties with the United States was changing Hawaii and determining its future. King Kalakaua had struggled to hold off the influence of the *Haoles*, or Caucasians, but he had been a weak leader. When Liliuokalani took the throne, she was determined to prevent the Americans from gaining any more strength, knowing that American sugar planters wanted the United States to annex Hawaii in order to ensure a firm market for their product.

After assuming power in 1891, she made sweeping changes in all branches of government. In January 1892, she threw out the old cabinet and proclaimed a new constitution. The new document restored many of the royal powers her brother had bargained away. Several American businessmen moved quickly to turn legislators against the queen. By the following year, a small group of Americans and Europeans, aided by United

States Marines, took over the Hawaiian government. Sanford B. Dole, a Honolulu-born American lawyer, was made governor of the Provisional Government of Hawaii. Unable to stop the overthrow of her kingdom, Queen Liliuokalani was placed under house arrest.

In 1898 Hawaii was formally annexed by the United States. The former queen retired from public life to write her memoirs, *Hawaii's Story by Hawaii's Queen*, and record the history and traditions of Hawaii in song.

All the members of Liliuokalani's family were musically talented; however, she was the most gifted of them all. At four she was able to sight read music and had perfect pitch. As she developed musically, she mixed Western melodies with Hawaiian instruments, such as piano, ukulele, guitar, zither, and organ.

Composing music seemed to come naturally to her. In 1866 she wrote the Hawaiian National Anthem, "He Mele Lahui Hawaii." Another favorite piece, "Aloha Oe" ("Farewell to Thee"), written in 1878, became the first Hawaiian song to become popular outside the islands.

Although Hawaii's political problems may have caused Liliuokalani great bitterness and distress throughout her lifetime, Hawaiian music, and Liliuokalani's contribution to its preservation, gave her life meaning and enriched the world.

Charles Edward King
Composer, Publisher, Bandleader
1879–1950

Because of his deep appreciation of Hawaiian traditions, Charles Edward King introduced Hawaiian music to the West without altering its purity.

Born in Honolulu, Hawaii, in 1874, Charles King was only one-quarter Hawaiian, yet his roots were planted deeply in Hawaiian culture. Queen Emma, wife of William Lunalilo, King of Hawaii in 1873, was his godmother, and Queen Liliuokalani was his own personal music teacher.

Charles attended the Kamehameha Schools, where he became fluent in the Hawaiian language and passionate about its literature and lore. Queen Liliuokalani, whose brief reign ended when Charles was still a teenager, had a deep influence on him and his attitude toward Hawaiian music. A noted composer herself, the Queen was instrumental in Charles's decision to follow the royal style of music, which embraced three standards: the lyrics must be Hawaiian, the subject should be about Hawaii, and the melody should be soft and slow.

As with most aspects of Hawaiian life in the late nineteenth and early twentieth centuries, however, the difficulty Hawaiians faced was to enhance what was uniquely Hawaiian, yet not completely reject all things American. The mainlanders, King knew, liked their music "jazzed-up," but how could he add pep to Hawaiian music without changing what made it Hawaiian? Throughout his professional life, King would address this dilemma.

After finishing college in New York, King returned to Hawaii and began teaching music composition in the public schools. As he taught, he continued developing his own talents, gradually going beyond the royal standard teachings of Queen Liliuokalani. His first hit song, "Na Lei O Hawai'i," brought him public acclaim. King concentrated on performance and composition. He played several instruments, including the steel guitar, ukulele, and violin. His many achievements included conductor of the Royal Hawaiian Band and writer of the opera *Prince of Hawaii*.

During King's later years, he devoted himself to music publication and television. He published *King's Book of Hawaiian Melodies* and *King's Songs of Hawaii* — two works that did the most to promote his reputation as the "dean" of Hawaiian music.

In the 1940s, Mr. King moved to New York City, where he ran a successful music publishing business. There he made a series of television tapes that featured Hawaiian music, which was becoming the latest rage. Charles King eventually produced more than forty tapes and had just composed the hit song "Television Hula" shortly before his death in 1950.

Mary Kawena Pukui
Author, Translator, Editor
1895–1986

Ancient Hawaiians composed songs, chants, and poems in tribute to the splendid beauty and history of their country. That these songs have survived and are available today in written form, in both Hawaiian and English, is due primarily to the efforts of Mary Kawena Pukui, fondly referred to as "Hawaii's greatest treasure."

Born on the Big Island of Hawaii in 1895, Mary Pukui was of Hawaiian, Samoan, and New England ancestry. Early in life she became interested in Hawaiian mythology and the art of *hula*, a means of storytelling using dancing and chanting. According to legend, hula artists must prove their mastery of chanting at Ka-ulu-a Paoa, Kauai — a place at the edge of the sea where they chant a *mele*, or song, so that it can be heard above the pounding waves and forceful winds. Although Mary never passed this rigorous test, she continued to honor the ancient tradition.

As Mary grew older, she immersed herself in reading the works of nineteenth century Hawaiian poets. Concerned that the ever-growing American influences in her country might alter its literary traditions, she dedicated herself to translating and preserving them. She began working with Laura Green, a missionary's daughter who also wanted to preserve ancient Hawaiian texts. Together they worked on several volumes that were published during the 1920s. These included *Hawaiian Stories and Wise Sayings*, *Folk Tales from Hawaii*, and *Legends of Kawaelo*.

Ms. Pukui was the sole author of *Hawaiian Folk Tales* (1933) and was the senior author of the *Hawaiian Dictionary and Place Names of Hawaii*. Perhaps her most important work is *The Echo of Our Song: Chants and Poems of the Hawaiians*, which she wrote with Alfons K. Korn in 1973.

Mary Kawena Pukui lived a long life, which she made richer by her studies and writings. In many ways her life was like the song she chanted at the edge of Ka-ulu-a Paoa as a little girl:

> *Laka dwells in beautiful forest,*
> *Standing alone at Moohelaia,*
> *An ohia tree standing up Maunaloa,*
> *Love to you, O Kaulana-ula*
> *Here is the voice, a gentle voice,*
> *A gentle chant of affection to you, O, Laka,*
> *Laka, inspire us.*[5]

Pablo Manlapit
Filipino Labor Leader
1891–1969

Filipino American workers of the early twentieth century differed from their Chinese and Japanese counterparts in one important way. When the United States took possession of the Philippine Islands after the Spanish-American War in 1898, the American government granted all Filipinos the status of American nationals. This meant that they would have most rights as U. S. citizens, except the rights to vote and legally become citizens.

Because the Philippines was a U. S. protectorate, the U. S. government funded the education of Filipino children. They studied English and American history and culture. Later, when Filipino workers came to America seeking opportunity, they considered themselves Americans coming to the mainland. Unfortunately, as soon as they arrived, Filipinos met with prejudice and discrimination. Feeling betrayed, many were outraged by their treatment. A few men, like Pablo Manlapit, expressed their anger openly and began to organize workers to gain their rights.

Pablo Manlapit was born in 1891 in Lipa, Batangas, in the Philippines. After completing a few years of high school, he headed for Hawaii in 1910. In Hawaii, Manlapit went to work for the Hawaiian Sugar Planter's Association. His energy and hard work gained him quick promotions until his boss discovered that he was involved in a labor dispute. Then he was fired immediately.

Manlapit then left the plantation and moved to Hilo, where he started two newspapers and opened a pool hall. Later, while working as a janitor in a law office, he decided to study law. In 1919 he became the first Filipino in Hawaii to pass the bar examination. Manlapit used his skills as a lawyer to become a formidable foe of the plantation owners. In August 1919 he established the Filipino Federation of Labor and the following year organized the Filipino Higher Wage Movement to improve living conditions among Filipino plantation workers. He worked tirelessly to increase workers wages from 72 cents to $1.25 for an eight-hour day; acquire overtime pay for work on Sundays and holidays; and gain maternity leave with pay for women laborers from two weeks before to six weeks after giving birth. When the planters' association flatly rejected these demands, Manlapit called for a strike. On January 19, 1920, more than 3,000 Filipino and Japanese workers went on strike.

Sugar plantation owners fought hard to squelch the strike and eventually evicted 12,000 workers from plantation houses. The Hawaiian Sugar Planter's Association then called in strike breakers and tried to prevent the workers' children from attending the local school. The pressure placed on the strikers was so great that, by the summer of 1920, all but 500 workers returned to work. Altogether the strike lasted 165 days.

Between 1920 and 1924, Manlapit continued to organize workers. In April 1924, another strike took place on Oahu. This became the bloodiest day of labor unrest in Hawaii's history. Sixteen strikers and four policemen were killed in a skirmish that was called the Hanapepe Massacre.

Pablo Manlapit received a stiff prison sentence for his involvement in the incident but fled into exile rather than serve time. He resurfaced in Hawaii in 1932 and formed the Filipino Labor Union. By 1935, however, he was again on the run. This time he left Hawaii for good and lived out his life in the Philippines.

Carlos Bulosan
Writer
1911–1956

"We arrived in Seattle on a June day. My first sight of the approaching land was an exhilarating experience. Everything seemed native and promising to me. It was like coming home after a long voyage, although as yet I had no home in this city." So wrote Carlos Bulosan remembering his first sight, in 1930, of the America that was to be his home for the rest of his short life.

The Philippine Islands, which Carlos Bulosan had just left, had been a colonial territory of the United States since 1898, when the islands were ceded to the United States at the end of the Spanish-American War. Carlos, unlike Asians from elsewhere, came to America as a United States "national." That means that Filipino workers in the United States, or *pinoys*, as they are often called, had most of the rights and privileges of United States citizens, although they could not vote in American elections.

Carlos was born in 1911 in the village of Binalonan in Pangasinan province. His parents were not poor by local standards; they had managed to put two sons through high school. Although Carlos did not graduate from high school before he left for the United States mainland, he did spend a year or two in school where he first demonstrated his writing talent in English on the school newspaper.

Prior to the Americans coming to the Philippines, the islands had been a colony of Spain, and Spanish was the language of education and the small educated class. By the time Carlos attended school, however, English had become the language of education in the Philippines. His textbooks were filled with stories of American heroes such as Presidents Washington and Lincoln and the ideals of American democracy. He pledged allegiance to the American flag each day and was taught that he was the equal of any American anywhere. Carlos, like all Filipinos, could freely come and go to the United States mainland. They were not restricted by immigration laws like other Asians were.

Because the life of a Philippine farmer was hard, it is not surprising that in the 1920s and 1930s, thousands of young men left home looking for fortune in the United States. The idea that you could get rich quick in the United States was reinforced by the stories told by returning pinoys who wore fancy clothes and flashed extra cash. Letters from America were always optimistic, too.

Driven by the lure of America, Carlos's parents sold a portion of their land to raise the $75.00 for Carlos's passage as they had for his two brothers before him. At the age of nineteen, he left his family and the familiar countryside to join the tens of thousands of his countrymen who had already sailed to America.

Although there had been no legal barriers to Carlos's coming into the United States, once he arrived in Seattle, Washington, he came face to face with the ugly realities of American racism. It was hard to accept the fact that the equality and opportunity he had dreamed of in America, indeed had been taught existed there, were not available to pinoys. Although he had been taught to think of himself as American, he found he was not accepted as one.

Bulosan later wrote, "I know deep down in my heart that I am an exile in America." For him, this sense of being an exile lead to his sense of guilt. "I feel like a criminal running away from a crime I did not commit," he would say. "And this crime is that I am a Filipino in America."

California laws as well as many other state laws discriminated against pinoys. They were not allowed to marry white women; they were disqualified from many jobs; and they were only allowed to live in segregated parts of cities. Pinoys could be cannery workers, diswashers, house servants, or farm laborers, but little else. As a pinoy, Bulosan drifted from one job to the next and from one unemployment line to another. He joined the body of homeless men who followed the harvest from southern California to Washington State to Alaska and back. As job conditions worsened, Filipino laborers began to organize into labor unions to try and change things.

Carlos Bulosan threw his whole support behind the labor movement and the "progressive forces" that drove it. Soon he began writing about it. He published his first book of poems in America in 1932. From then on, writing was to be his major occupation.

Bulosan lived with his brother Aurelio in Los Angeles, and spent much of his time in the public library where he read extensively. By 1934 his writing began to gain prominence. Then in 1936, it seemed his world began to fall apart. He came down with tuberculosis and spent the next two years in Los Angeles County Hospital recuperating. He continued to read and to write. From his hospital bed he followed reports of World War II erupting in Spain, Europe, and Northeast Asia.

When the United States entered the war in 1941 and the Japanese invaded the Philippines, the attitude toward those of Philippine ancestry seemed to change. Once scorned and ignored, now they were suddenly welcomed as comrades in the fight against dictators of the world. This change, in part, led to a greater interest in the works of Carlos Bulosan. He published two books of poetry — *Letter from America* in 1942 and *Voice of Bataan* in 1943. The following year, his best known book, *Laughter of My Father*, was published.

The book Carlos is best remembered for today, *America Is in the Heart*, was published in 1946. It is an autobiographical novel in which he tells the story of the Filipino in America. And while he describes all the heartbreaks and frustrations, all the racism that faced the pinoy, the book ends with praise for America. It is not the America of racist oppression that is the real America, he says. Rather, the real America is still the America of his Philippine dreams, the ideal America that is in the heart.

> "I glanced out of the window again to look at the broad land I had dreamed so much about, only to discover with astonishment that the American earth was like a huge heart unfolding warmly to receive me . . . . It came to me that no man — no one at all — could destroy my faith in America again. It was something that had grown out of my defeats and successes, something shaped by my struggles for a place in this vast land . . . . It was something that grew out of the sacrifices and loneliness of my friends, of my brothers in America and my family in the Philippines — something that grew out of our desire to know America and to become a part of her great tradition, and to contribute something toward her final fulfillment. I knew that no man could destroy my faith in America that had sprung from all our hopes and aspiration, ever."[6]

Bulosan was thirty-five years old when *America Is in the Heart* was first published. Ten years later, he died in Seattle, the city that had welcomed him to America. He died a young man in a body old before its time. In his final years he had continued to fight for the ideal America, working closely with the Filipino labor union, ILWU Local 37 where, among other things, he edited the yearbook and wrote poetry. Some thirty years later, a committee made up of Filipino community members, former friends, and University of Washington students erected a tombstone at Bulosan's grave. The epitaph comes from one of his unpublished poems:

> *Here, here the tomb of Bulosan is:*
> *Here, here also are his words,*
> *dry as the grass is.*

D.T. Suzuki
Philosopher, Teacher
1870–1966

During most of the last twenty years of his life, D.T. Suzuki lived in New York City. He could have lived in Japan, where he was considered a national treasure. But New York was a youthful place, he felt, and he loved its energy. Many Americans knew and admired this scholarly man, who had spent his long life explaining the mysteries of Eastern religion to the West, and they allowed him great freedom.

Daisetz Teitaro Suzuki was born into a family of physicians in 1870 in Kanazawa, Japan. It was assumed he, too, would enter medical practice, but the untimely death of his father made the cost of a full-time university education impossible. Instead, Daisetz spent much of his time at a nearby Zen monastery, studying Buddhism with an honored teacher.

It was his Zen master and teacher who introduced young Daisetz to the publishing world in the United States. On his teacher's recommendation, the young twenty-seven-year-old was hired as a translator by Open Court, a small publishing company in LaSalle, Illinois. He moved there and collaborated with Dr. Paul Carus, a noted scholar of oriental philosophy. Together they translated several books from the Chinese, which were published in the early 1900s.

These books, including the works of Tao Te Ching and a volume called *Awakening of Faith,* helped Westerners grasp the differences between their religions and those of the East. Zen, for example, is a branch of Buddhism that was developed in China around 600 A.D. and later brought to Japan, where it had a profound influence on the culture. Zen (from the Japanese *zazen*, meaning "to sit and meditate") strives to free the mind of useless clutter. Through quiet reflection the practitioner of Zen seeks enlightenment — in other words, the ability to understand what is true and meaningful in the world.

D.T. Suzuki left Illinois in 1908 and traveled to Europe. There he lectured at various universities and became famous for his role as both interpreter of Eastern religious ideas for the West and Western religious ideas for the East. In 1909 he returned to Tokyo to teach English at the Imperial University. Later he moved to Kyoto's Otani University where he was a professor of both English and Buddhist philosophy.

Professor Suzuki's opposition to the Japanese military buildup before and during World War II led him to spend most of the early 1940s under house arrest. He continued writing, however, and his books, such as *Introduction to Zen Buddhism* and *Essays in Zen Buddhism*, became classics in the field of comparative religion.

In 1951 Suzuki moved to New York City, where he lived until just before his death in 1966. During that time he held posts of visiting professor at Columbia University and the University of Mexico. Until well into his nineties, he amazed his younger friends and colleagues by flying around the world lecturing at Oxford, Cambridge, and Munich as well as Stanford, Chicago, and Harvard.

D. T. Suzuki became a living example of the doctrine he preached. As one observer noted: "Dr Suzuki is obviously a man who thought everything out long ago and has reached a state of certainty. The certainty, it appears, is so profound that it needs no emphasis . . . ."

Philip Vera Cruz
Labor Leader
1904

Philip Vera Cruz was born on Christmas Day, 1904, in a small barrio called Saoang, in the province of Ilocos Sur, which is on the island of Luzon in the Philippines. Twenty-two years later, in 1926, he arrived in Seattle, Washington, in search of a better life.

He came for the reason other young Filipino men had come — to work, save money, and support their families. Soon after arriving in America, however, they learned just how difficult it would be to achieve their goals. As Philip Cruz remembered, "All the stories we heard were only success stories. So my plan was to finish college in America, get a good job over there, save my money, and then return home and support my family. It was only after I finally got to America that I understood how different reality was for us Filipinos."

Filipino men learned that reality meant low-paying jobs and racial discrimination. Conditions such as these led Filipino Americans who were working in the fields and canneries in Hawaii and on the West Coast of the United States to organize into unions to protect their rights and get better wages. Throughout the 1920s labor organizers such as Pablo Manlapit struggled to acquire better working conditions on the Hawaiian Islands. Others, such as Chris Mensalves, Ernesto Mangaoang, and Larry Itliong, worked on the mainland throughout the 1930s and 1960s to improve the quality of life for Filipino workers.

It was during the Filipino American farm laborers' strike in the asparagus fields of Stockton, California, that Philip Cruz first met Chris Mensalves. And it was there that he first dedicated himself to the cause of Filipino labor rights. Although Philip would like to have stayed on to help the union, he was financially desperate. Feeling obligated to help support his family, especially his younger brother who was in law school in Manila, Philip went on to Alaska to work in a salmon cannery.

In Alaska, workers were protected by a strong union. Conditions and pay were better than California standards. But work only lasted for two summer months. So it was back to California — to Delano where grapes needed to be picked. By that time the Stockton strike was over. Although the strike had brought Filipino American workers together, it would take another twenty years before they would unite again in such numbers for a common cause. This time it would be in the grape fields south of Stockton — in Delano, California.

For the next twenty years, Philip Vera Cruz continued traveling with migrant groups, working at seasonal jobs in fields and canneries throughout the western United States. On September 8, 1965, in Delano, he joined others in a grape strike that sparked the great farm workers movement of the 1960s and led to the historic formation of the United Farm Workers (UFW), under the charismatic leadership of Cesar Chavez.

During this strike Philip became an officer of the UFW. In 1971 he became its vice president, a position he held until his resignation in 1977. In 1987 he was awarded the first Ninoy M. Aquino Award for lifelong service to the Filipino community in America. The award included a trip back to the Philippines, the first he had made since leaving there sixty years before. There he was reunited with the family he had worked so hard to support over the years. As he later recalled, "My brother and sister got good educations and they succeeded in providing their children with a good education. That's important to me because I made it possible for them."

Philip Vera Cruz came to the United States to work, save money, and support his family. He achieved this goal and more. His efforts have helped change history and improve the lives of thousands in the process. He continues to offer others a great challenge.

> "If I could inspire one or two young people to be successful by hearing my story. . . ." he says, "if this one or two young people might turn into someone who could help change history, why that would be good! . . . If more young people could just get involved in the important issues of social justice, they would form a golden foundation for the struggle of all people to improve their lives."[7]

Chiura Obata

Painter

1888–1975

My aim is to create a bowl full of joy
*   clear as the sky*
*   pure as falling cherry petals*
Without worry, without doubt;
Then comes full energy, endless power
And the road to art.[8]

— Chiura Obata, Topaz, 1943

When Chiura Obata was eighteen and about to be drafted into the Japanese army, he left his homeland for California. He arrived in San Francisco in 1906, only intending to stay a short time before heading for Europe where he would study painting. A side trip to Yosemite and the High Sierras in California, however, so fired his artistic imagination that he decided to postpone his trip east.

Chiura began studying art at the University of California, Berkeley. After receiving his degree, he began teaching at the university. From 1931 to 1957 he was a professor of art. His long tenure was interrupted only briefly when he, like other Japanese Americans on the West Coast, was sent to a government detention camp following the Japanese bombing of Pearl Harbor in Hawaii in 1941.

Although neither the FBI nor military intelligence at the time officially considered the Japanese American population a threat to national security, the U. S. government began relocating all people of Japanese ancestry who were living on the West Coast to makeshift camps on remote, unused federal lands.

Chiura Obata joined other first- and second-generation Japanese Americans first at Tanforan, and then at Topaz, Utah — one of ten detention camps designed to house the Japanese for the duration of World War II.

Chiura Obata believed strongly that he and his fellow artists in the detention camps should continue their work, no matter how bad the conditions. He organized art schools for both adults and children and used his connections at the University of California to have materials shipped to the camp in Topaz. Since no cameras were allowed in camp, Professor Obata hoped that paintings would provide a permanent record of camp life that could be passed on to future generations. The results are stunningly beautiful depictions of this tragic desert exile.

"Hatsuki Wakasa Shot by MP" (Topaz, April 11, 1943), watercolor by Chiura Obata

Although Professor Obata was instrumental in inspiring many during his stay at Topaz, his political views angered some fellow Japanese internees. Obata was considered "pro-American" in his views. One night following a political disagreement with another inmate, Obata was hit over the head with an iron pipe. He was rushed to a hospital in Salt Lake City and from there moved to St. Louis, a location that was considered a "safe risk" by the U. S. government. Obata and his family remained in St. Louis until after the war, when they returned to Berkeley.

In *Beyond Words*, a book of drawings and writings depicting life in the Japanese American concentration camps, Professor Obata is remembered as one who looked for the best in the dismal surroundings and encouraged others not to despair. As his wife Haruko wrote:

> "It (Topaz) was a totally different environment from what we were used to in Berkeley — dry and hot. There were scorpions, too. We never had seen those before. The sunsets were beautiful though. Everybody was always complaining but Chiura would say, 'Just look around. . . . We will survive if we forget the sands at our feet and look to the mountains for inspiration.' "[9]

A Japanese family awaiting internment in a detention camp in 1942

Inmates in America's Detention Camps

1942–1945

On February 19, 1942, just two months after the United States went to war with the Japanese following their bombing of Pearl Harbor in Hawaii, President Franklin Delano Roosevelt signed Executive Order 9066. It authorized military authorities to remove all people of Japanese ancestry living on the West Coast and incarcerate them in camps set up in remote areas of the country for the duration of the war. The order, which directly affected about 113,000 Japanese Americans, 80,000 of whom were American citizens, was later judged racially motivated and a violation of their constitutional rights. This judgment, however, came too late to correct the wrongs that have had lasting consequences even to the present day.

Notices ordering the removal of Japanese Americans were posted on walls and buildings, printed in newspapers, and announced on the radio. The head of each family was ordered to report to a Civil Control Center to pick up numbered tags that were to be worn by each member of the family and attached to the two suitcases and one dufflebag that they were allowed to bring to the camps. All other belongings had to be sold, stored, or thrown away. Many families had to sell their houses and businesses. Each had a week to get ready, but had no idea how long they would be imprisoned during the war.

Japanese reactions to removal varied widely. While most felt they had no real alternative but to accept the executive order, others resisted imprisonment, and a few actually challenged its constitutionality in court.

Fearing that total opposition to removal might lead to violence and bloodshed, the Japanese American Citizens League (JACL) advised Japanese to cooperate, "under protest," with the order. Most did. In fact, most people believed that cooperating with the government edict was the best way to help the country at the time.

As dazed Japanese Americans prepared, the U. S. government began building the detention camps on unused federal lands in remote desert or swamp areas. Eventually, there were ten detention camps: Topaz in Utah, Poston and Gila in Arizona, Manzanar and Tule Lake in California, Minidoka in Idaho, Granada in Colorado, Rohwer and Jerome in Arkansas, and Heart Mountain in Wyoming. Each camp housed between 5,000 and 20,000 Issei (Japanese immigrants who were restricted by U. S. law from becoming U. S. citizens.) and Nisei (children of Japanese immigrants who were born in the United States and, therefore, citizens).

Thousands of Japanese Americans on their way toward trains that will carry them to detention camps

Before moving to the camps, angry, frightened Japanese Americans were taken to makeshift assembly centers near large cities. These quarters were former fairgrounds, racetracks, or livestock halls, where animal stalls were quickly cleaned and painted for human occupancy.

By the summer of 1942, permanent camps were completed and Japanese Americans were transported there by train. Upon arriving at the camps, they were shocked to find row upon row of black tar-paper barracks the size of chicken houses surrounded by endless barbed-wire fences patrolled by armed soldiers. In western camps, such as those in Utah, California, and Arizona, people would have to suffer through hot dusty summers and below-zero winters. In southern camps, they would have to contend with damp, swampy lowlands and hot, humid temperatures.

The camp at Manzanar, California

As the initial shock of the primitive camps began to wear off and imprisonment became a way of life, people began organizing schools, health clinics, recreational facilities, and a governing board. Work projects were started, and a certain camp routine was established.

Although camps took on the activities of small, self-sufficient towns, there was nothing normal about camp life. The conditions were terrible: five to eight people lived in bare, 20 x 25 foot (6 x 8 meter) rooms with no privacy. Three hundred inmates shared a mess hall, laundry, showers, latrine, and recreation hall. Until inmates began taking responsibility for life in the camps, food was bad, and boredom a constant problem.

In the midst of all the tension and frustration, camps had to run smoothly and basic services had to be provided. Some camps grew their own food. In larger camps, factories were set up. Because families were given only $7.50 a month as an allowance, people needed to work just to earn enough money for necessities. The pay scale was $12.00, $16.00, and $19.00.

The most valued jobs were those connected to release programs, which contracted Nisei men out to farmers who needed laborers to harvest crops. These jobs allowed men the freedom to be outside the camps. Young people also were allowed temporary release from camps to attend college.

By February 1943, some young Nisei men were volunteering from the camp to fight in World War II in an elite, all-Japanese American regiment called the 442nd Regimental Combat Team. The team, which had been established as an experimental regiment composed of second-generation Japanese Americans and white officers, would eventually become one of the most highly decorated units of the war. Nisei distinguished themselves as scouts and as interpreters in the Pacific War and as an elite fighting machine in both the Pacific and European fronts. Often volunteering against the wishes of their parents and under criticism of many camp elders, Nisei believed that by serving in the war, they would win freedom for their families and eliminate prejudice against Japanese Americans.

Japanese workers in a release program

Due to the valiant fighting of Nisei soldiers and gradual changes in the attitudes of American people, Japanese Americans slowly began regaining some of what racial discrimination and greed had unjustly taken from them. In December 1944, pending court cases were decided in favor of releasing Japanese American evacuees. Based on those decisions, and on the fact that the U. S. military no longer considered mass exclusion of West Coast Japanese necessary, it was announced that all the camps would be closed by the end of 1945.

At this time, more than 30,000 people had already left the camps. By September 1945, about 15,000 people a month were leaving. Although most people were happy to finally regain their freedom, many protested the sudden closings of the camps. Those who had had to sell their farms and homes when the government imprisoned them, now had nowhere to go.

Anti-Japanese signs often appeared in public places during World War II.

Many feared anti-Japanese treatment when they returned to their communities. Having already suffered mentally and financially, Japanese Americans rightly believed they should be given some type of government assistance. Their petitions were ignored, however, and they had to relocate on their own, with minimal assistance from the government.

Their struggle for compensation for wrongful imprisonment and loss of material gain continued until well into the 1980s. In the summer and fall of 1981, the Commission on Wartime Relocation and Internment of Civilians (CWRIC) held hearings on the imprisonment of Japanese Americans during World War II and concluded:

> "The promulgation of Executive Order 9066 was not justified by military necessity, and the decisions which followed from it — detention, ending detention and ending exclusion — were not driven by analysis of military conditions. The broad historical causes which shaped these decisions were race prejudice, war hysteria and a failure of political leadership . . . ."[10]

In August 1988, President Ronald Reagan signed a bill that offered an official apology to American citizens of Japanese ancestry and gave a payment of $20,000 to each survivor of the detention camps. He said that the imprisonment of Japanese Americans had been "a grave wrong" and the time had come to finish "a sad chapter in American history." It is, indeed, a sad chapter, for such grave wrongs can never be made right.

"Keep-Away Sign at Topaz" (1943), watercolor by Chiura Obata

A Case Against the
Internment of Japanese Americans

On April 30, 1942, General John L. De Witt issued the order that all persons of Japanese ancestry (American citizens as well as resident aliens of Japanese ancestry) were under immediate curfew and should await orders for removal to detention camps. Most obeyed without hesitation. Believing that cooperating with the government edict was the best way to help the country at the time, the Japanese American Citizens League (JACL) advised Japanese Americans to comply.

Three men in three different states, however, refused to obey the order and were sent to prison: Gordon Hirabayashi of Washington, Fred Korematsu of California, and Minoru Yasui of Oregon. Forty years later, their convictions were overturned. Investigations in the 1980s by the Congressional Commission on Wartime Relocation and Internment of Civilians led to the conclusion that the U. S. government not only had omitted giving pertinent information to the Supreme Court concerning these cases, but also misled the Supreme Court on matters of the "military necessity issue."

Gordon Hirabayashi, a native of Seattle, was a student at the University of Washington in 1942. During the first week or so of the 8:00 PM to 6:00 AM curfew, he dutifully rushed back from the library or work to his dorm. After a few days, however, he began to feel there was no reason he should have to be inside at 8:00 when none of his dormmates were similarly affected. Believing that the principles of the Bill of Rights supported his decision to ignore orders that singled him out just because of his ethnic background, Hirabayashi began ignoring the curfew. He was prepared to go to prison rather than obey the orders.

Meanwhile in Portland, Oregon, a young lawyer named Minoru Yasui was making a similar decision. Guided by his own legal training, he reasoned that the curfew and internment orders were simply against the law. After talking with other attorneys and the Japanese American Citizens League, he decided to resist the order. On March 28, Yasui had a friend call the police and tell them he was not obeying the curfew. The police tried to ignore Yasui, who eventually walked into a Portland police station and forced the arrest. He intended to use his entire life savings of $5,000 to see his case through court.

Fred Korematsu's reasons for disobeying the army's orders were different still. He had no particular moral or legal qualms. He simply didn't want to leave his Oakland, California, home for "personal" reasons. He, too, was arrested, tried, convicted, and eventually sent to prison.

In May of 1943, Gordon Hirabayashi's appeal was heard by the U. S. Supreme Court. In June, the eight justices handed down their decision, agreeing unanimously with the ruling of the Washington State court. They felt that "national safety" concerns were, at the time, more pressing than issues of racial discrimination. The courts reached the same conclusions in the cases of Korematsu and Yasui.

In 1981, however, all three men were told by a lawyer at the University of California, San Diego, that evidence had been uncovered suggesting that in 1942, the War Department had deliberately changed the wording of its original evacuation order. The difference seemed minor; but to legal scholars it was significant enough to make the cases worth retrying.

Two years later, courts in California and Oregon dismissed both the Korematsu and Yasui cases after "vacating" the original convictions. A judge in Seattle, however, decided not to dismiss the case against Gordon Hirabayashi. Instead, he handed down an important ruling, saying that because the War Department changed the wording of General De Witt's original order, the court cases had never been pleaded correctly. The judge left open the possibility that the evacuation order might have been found illegal and stopped by the Supreme Court.

The legal battles of Fred Korematsu, Gordon Hirabayashi, and Minoru Yasui helped to uncover the truth about a racially motivated period in U. S. history and correct the political and legal mistakes that were perpetuating discrimination. Their efforts contributed to the passage of legislation that eventually compensated, though never adequately, for Japanese American losses. In 1948 Congress passed the Japanese American Evacuation Claims Act that appropriated funds to reimburse Japanese Americans for their losses. President Ford issued Presidential Proclamation 4417 in 1976 rescinding Executive Order 9066 and apologizing for it. Finally, Congress passed the Civil Liberties Act of 1988, authorizing compensation for living surviviors of the camps.

Gordon Hirabayashi testifying before The Commission on Wartime Relocation and Internment of Civilians

Men of the 442nd training at Camp Shelby, Mississippi

The 442nd Combat Regiment

1942–1945

After the Japanese bombing of Pearl Harbor on December 7, 1941, Japanese Americans living on the West Coast were viewed with suspicion. Giving in to widespread fear and prejudice, the U. S. government decided that anyone with a Japanese surname was untrustworthy. After Executive Order No. 9066 was issued in February 1942, the Army ordered the evacuation of 120,000 people of Japanese descent from their homes and their incarceration in camps for the duration of the war.

Young Japanese American men, second generation Nisei, wanted to prove their loyalty to the United States. As a result of their petitions for induction into the Army and the need to have Japanese-speaking soldiers, President Franklin D. Roosevelt agreed to establish a volunteer, all-Nisei regiment. Recruiting turned out to be easy, though not without some criticism from the Japanese community; nearly 10,000 young men in Hawaii alone answered the call.

In September 1943, the 100th Infantry Battalion, made up of former members of the Hawaiian National Guard plus new recruits, landed at Salerno, Italy. They joined the fight to liberate territory held by German troops on the road to Rome. Within six months, 600 of the 1,400 soldiers who had fought in Italy were dead.

In June 1944, the 442nd Regimental Combat Team — made up of Nisei from Hawaii and Japanese Americans from the detention camps — arrived in Europe to join the 100th Infantry. They were assigned to rescue the lost battalion of the 36th Texas Division of the U. S. Army — 211 men completely surrounded by the Germans in France's Vosges Mountains. After six days of fierce fighting and heavy casualties (some units of the 442nd lost 60% of their troops), the Lost Battalion was rescued. As one soldier from the 36th Texas Division remembered: "The Germans hit us from one flank, then the other, then the front and the rear. . . . We were never so glad to see anyone as those fighting Japanese Americans."

Nisei men also served in Pacific combat areas, home-front intelligence units, and government information services. As language and intelligence specialists, they uncovered many of Japan's battle plans before they got underway. Nisei women served as WACs (Women's Auxiliary Corps).

A machine gunner of the 100th Battalion in Italy

When the war was over, Japanese American men and women were honored for service to their country. There were 18,143 individual decorations — including one Congressional Medal of Honor (for Private Sadao S. Munemori, who was killed saving two fellow soldiers near Seravezza, Italy) — 47 Distinguished Service Crosses, 350 Silver Stars, 810 Bronze Stars, and 3,600 Purple Hearts.

On July 15, 1946, President Harry Truman welcomed the surviving Nisei soldiers of the 442nd. "You fought for the free nations of the world," he told them. ". . . you fought not only the enemy, you fought prejudice — and you won."

Winning did not mean the same thing for everyone, however. While Japanese American soldiers were dying to win back freedom for Europeans, many of their own families were imprisoned by the U. S. government at home and denied freedom because of race. When Japanese American soldiers returned from the war, many found that their families were still being held in detention camps, and they could only visit them in the presence of armed guards.

Private Tsukio Yamagato of the 100/442 being awarded a Purple Heart

Sessue (Kintaro) Hayakawa

Film star
1890–1973

At the height of his acting career, Sessue (Kintaro) Hayakawa had dined with two American presidents and was the proud owner of a mansion in Hollywood and a gold-plated Pierce-Arrow car. That, however, was during the silent movie era, when Hayakawa's handsome face and box-office appeal made him much in demand by film producers across the country. When the talkie era began, Sessue Hayakawa lost his box-office appeal. By the 1930s, his career in Hollywood was all but over.

An acting career was the last thing Kintaro's parents would have wanted for their son. ("Sessue" was the name the young actor used in Hollywood.) The Hayakawas were aristocrats with family roots in Japan's Chiba province that could be traced as far back as two thousand years. Kintaro's father, who once was a provincial governor, had brought up his sons according to the strict warrior code of the samurai.

Even Kintaro's plans did not include acting. As a teenager, he wanted to become a naval officer. He entered the Navy Preparatory School in Tokyo, where he graduated four years later. Following graduation, he was accepted by the Naval Academy in Etajima. That summer, however, he ruptured an eardrum while diving and was disqualified from entering the academy. Totally humiliated by this unfortunate turn of events, Kintaro attempted suicide.

He recovered from the self-inflicted stab wounds, however, and a year later traveled to the United States where he enrolled at the University of Chicago. Kintaro Hayakawa graduated in 1913 with a degree in political science and planned to return to Japan and enter public life. On his way home, however, he stopped in Los Angeles, where he attended a play staged by a small Japanese theatre company. That one event changed his life forever.

Kintaro went backstage after the performance and complained to the director that the performance was weak. He suggested that he could do much better. The director considered his bold offer and after some negotiation turned the company over to the brash young man. In 1914 Hayakawa's talented direction of the play *Typhoon* caught the attention of a Hollywood producer, who decided to make it into a motion picture starring the director himself.

Hayakawa's silent movie career took off. From 1915 through the 1920s, he was one of the most popular and highest-paid actors in Hollywood. He and his wife, Japanese actress Tsuru Aoki, socialized with many movie greats — Mary Pickford, Douglas Fairbanks, and Cecil B. DeMille. When the silent movies faded and talkies took their place, Hayakawa turned for a time to theatre. He toured the United States in several popular plays.

By the late 1930s, the Hayakawas were living in Paris, France. Sessue had made a few European films and was earning a living painting on silk. He and his wife were living modestly in the city, without a hint of the old Hollywood extravagance.

In 1940 the German army occupied Paris. Although Japan was an ally of Germany, Sessue remained on the side of the European countries and their allies. Because of Sessue's wartime stance, the Hayakawas did not return to Japan until long after the war's end. In 1949 they went back to the United States where Sessue starred in a major Hollywood film called *Tokyo Joe*. A year later, he and his wife returned to Japan where Sessue devoted himself to the study of Zen Buddhism, a religion that stresses meditation as a means of becoming enlightened. Eventually, he was chosen as a candidate for the priesthood and ordained in a traditional Zen Buddhist ceremony.

Hayakawa's life of peaceful reflection was interrupted in 1956 when he briefly returned to acting. After much soul-searching concerning his religious beliefs about war and peace, he accepted a Hollywood movie contract to play the role of the Japanese colonel in the movie *Bridge on the River Kwai.* The role eventually won him an acclaimed Oscar nomination for best supporting actor.

Scene from the movie Bridge on the River Kwai

Hayakawa made several more films before he returned to Japan in 1961 after the death of his wife. Once again, he immersed himself in Zen Buddhism, living the remainder of his life in a modest home in suburban Tokyo, near his three grown children.

Sessue Hayakawa's life, which was an expression of his spirituality and a wide range of artistic talents, enriched others. Some critics question his portrayal of the Asian American male as a stern, rigid disciplinarian. Others agree, however, that the ultimate test of a movie role model is not exclusively the image that is created on screen.

Yoshiko Uchida
Children's author
1921–1992

In her book *The Birthday Visitor*, Yoshiko Uchida tells of a seven-year-old girl named Emi Watanabe who is growing up between two very different cultures in Berkeley, California, during the 1920s.

Yoshiko Uchida draws on her own experiences growing up in Berkeley during the 1920s and 1930s to create such characters as Emi Watanabe. Her parents had both come to America from Japan and settled in the heart of Berkeley's Japanese community. As a child, Yoshiko knew many people like Mr. Wada, whom she loved dearly, but who also seemed more a part of the past than the future. Yoshiko, like many other second-generation Japanese Americans, struggled constantly to find her own way between her family's heritage and the new world to which she belonged. How was it possible to be part of both cultures?

After the bombing of Pearl Harbor on December 7, 1941, and America's declaration of war against Japan, hatred, fear, and suspicion of Japanese Americans living on the West Coast escalated. Many Japanese found themselves in the difficult position of having to renounce their ancestral homeland to prove their loyalty to the United States. By February 1942, Executive Order 9066 prescribed areas from which "any or all persons may be excluded." Although the word "Japanese" was not used, the order was directed solely at people of Japanese ancestry. It set in motion the forced removal of more than 100,000 Japanese Americans, the majority of whom were American citizens, from their homes and places of business. Although no evidence of disloyalty or sabotage on the part of Japanese Americans could be found, they were deprived of their rights and imprisoned in poorly equipped camps in isolated areas simply on the basis of their ancestry and under the guise of "military necessity."

Yoshiko was twenty on December 7, 1941, when, after studying for her final exams at the University of California library, she returned to her home to find that her father had been taken away by the FBI. After questioning, Mr. Uchida was taken to a prisoner-of-war camp in Missoula, Montana. Like other Japanese Americans, he lost his income and his home. His keys were confiscated by the government, including those to his bank deposit box, and use of his bank accounts was limited.

A few months after Mr. Uchida was imprisioned, Yoshiko, her sister Kay, and her mother learned that they had exactly ten days to report to the Civil Control Station, where they would be transported to the Tanforan Assembly Center in San Bruno, California. They were given numbered tags for all their belongings. From then on, they were simply known as Family Number 13453. The Uchidas had to sell, give away, or store all the belongings that they would not be able carry to the detention camp.

On May 1, 1942, the Uchidas were taken to the Tanforan racetrack with 8,000 other Japanese Americans. The racetrack, which the government had quickly converted into living areas, was surrounded by a barbed wire fence and guarded by armed soldiers in towers. Although the horse stables at Tanforan were meant to be only temporary housing, Yoshiko, Kay, and their mother would stay five months there. Each stable consisted of fifty stalls. Each family lived in a stall that was ten feet by twenty feet.

About a week after the Uchidas arrived at Tanforan, Mr. Uchida was transferred there to join them. Now they would have to crowd four cots into a stall that had housed a single horse. Soon after the Uchidas settled into the tiny shack, Yoshiko and Kay began teaching school.

In September, families were told to pack up their few belongings and be ready to move to a more permanent camp. The Uchidas were sent to the Central Utah Relocation Center in Topaz, Utah, which was a cluster of tar-paper barracks on the edge of the Sevier Desert.

At Topaz, Yoshiko and Kay resumed their teaching. The frequent dust storms, rain squalls, and severe snowstorms made one-room living almost unbearable. Of her terrible experience in the hot Utah desert, Yoshiko remembers mainly the dust, which swirled around the camp and poured into every crack in the barracks. Of the frequent dust storms, she wrote: ". . . the wind reached such force we thought our barrack would be torn from its feeble foundations. Pebbles and rocks rained against the walls. . . . The air was so thick with the smoke-like dust, my mouth was gritty with it and my lungs seemed penetrated by it. For hours the wind shrieked around our shuddering barrack . . . ."

In 1943 Yoshiko and her sister were able to leave Topaz. Kay was offered a position as an assistant in a nursery school. Yoshiko was allowed to attend graduate school at Smith College where she received a masters in education. She left the camp not depressed and discouraged but determined to prove that the Americans who discriminated against people of Japanese ancestry were wrong. "I felt a tremendous sense of responsibility to make good," she said, "not just for myself, but for all Japanese Americans. . . . It was sometimes an awesome burden to bear."

When the war ended, Yoshiko's parents left Topaz. Several years later, they were able to purchase a house in California, just two blocks from the one they had to leave before the war. Yoshiko, after receiving a fellowship to study in Japan for two years, traveled throughout the country, collecting folktales for her writing. She returned to the United States with a renewed sense of pride in her Japanese heritage.

With this new confidence and self-knowledge, she began writing books for young people. In all, Ms. Uchida wrote more than twenty-eight books.

In *The Birthday Visitor, A Jar of Dreams, The Best Bad Thing, The Happiest Ending,* and *The Samurai of Gold Hill,* she created stories and characters based on her own past. She describes her wartime experiences in *Journey to Topaz* and *Journey Home* and in the nonfiction book for adults, *Desert Exile.* Her writing brings important knowledge to all Americans. Her message was one of hope, pride, and perseverence at a time when discrimination, persecution, and imprisonment was a way of life.

Isamu Noguchi
Sculptor
1904–1988

The great artist and sculptor, Isamu Noguchi, resisted artistic boundaries and their limitations, and experimented freely with stone, metal, wood, paper, and clay.

Isamu was born in Los Angeles, California, in 1904. His Japanese father, Yone Noguchi, was a poet and art critic. His mother, Leonie Gilmour, was an American writer. At the time of Isamu's birth, his father had already abandoned his mother and returned to Japan. Two years later, Isamu and his mother left America and also moved to Japan. By this time, however, Yone Noguchi was well settled into a traditional marriage with a Japanese woman.

When Isamu was four or five, he and his mother moved to the seaside village of Chigasaki. In 1917 Isamu's mother decided that he should go to America to continue his education. She enrolled him in Interlaken, an experimental school in northern Indiana. At thirteen years of age, Isamu made the trip to the States alone and arrived in Rolling Prairie, Indiana, only to find that the school had been closed and its property taken over by the U.S. Army. Within the year, World War I ended and the training camp was closed. Isamu, having nowhere to go, joined two caretakers who were camping out in one of the deserted buildings.

Eventually, Isamu started attending the public school in the nearby town of Rolling Prarie. A year later, Dr. Edward A. Rumley, founder of

Interlaken, learned of Isamu's dilemma and found a family that would take him in.

After graduation, he apprenticed for a short time with Gutzon Borglum, an American sculptor best known for creating the Mount Rushmore National Memorial in South Dakota. The relationship between Borglum and Noguchi began to fail, however, shortly after Borglum told Noguchi that he would never become a true sculptor.

Disappointed by the rejection, Noguchi enrolled at New York's Columbia University in 1923, where he began studying medicine. In 1926, however, after seeing the exhibition of a Romanian sculptor, Constantin Brancusi, Noguchi decided to devote himself to art and discontinued his medical studies. A year later, he received a Guggenheim Fellowship, which would allow him to study in Paris, France.

In Paris, Noguchi met Brancusi, who, after a little persuasion, agreed to let him be his stonecutter. With Brancusi as his tutor, Noguchi learned to respect the materials and the tools of the sculptor. A few years later, he left Paris and traveled throughout Asia. He spent time in Peking, China, where he learned brush drawing. Later, he studied ceramics in Japan. By the time he returned to New York in the mid-1930s, his reputation as a sculptor was widely known.

Noguchi's fame spread nationally in 1938 when his design of a plaque was chosen for the new headquarters of the Associated Press at New York City's Rockefeller Center. The plaque, which he had convinced sponsors to let him make in stainless steel, was unveiled in 1940 with great ceremony. The year before, Noguchi had thrilled New Yorkers with his "strikingly modern" fountain, which he had designed for the New York World's Fair.

It appeared that Noguchi was well on his way in the art world. However, tragic world events in 1941 would reshape his life and force him to deal with the realities of his Japanese American citizenship.

On December 7, 1941, Japanese forces bombed Pearl Harbor in Hawaii.

President Franklin Roosevelt immediately ordered the internment of Japanese Americans living on the West Coast. Although Isamu Noguchi lived in New York and was considered a "safe Japanese," he voluntarily went with other Japanese Americans to an internment camp in Poston, Arizona. His intention was to lend his skills in building playgrounds and parks for the inmates of the camp. Noguchi's intentions, however, were not welcomed by the War Relocation Authority. When Noguchi realized that his presence was not wanted, he applied for release from the camp.

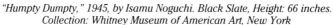

"Humpty Dumpty," 1945, by Isamu Noguchi. Black Slate, Height: 66 inches. Collection: Whitney Museum of American Art, New York

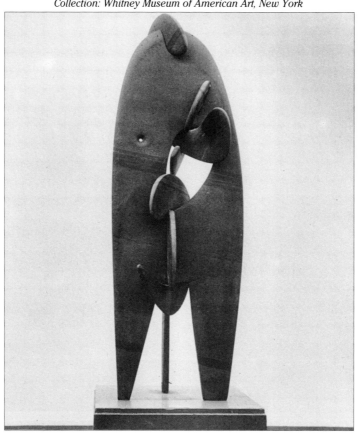

Following his release from Poston seven months later, Noguchi began producing his most serious work to date. In 1952 he moved to Japan, where he married Yoshiko (Shirley) Yamaguchi. From their home in Japan and from a studio that he maintained in New York, Noguchi produced a marvelous array of stone, metal, wood, and paper sculptures, many of which were installed in public places around the world. He also began designing the sculpture gardens, which are now prominent in such cities as New York, Houston, Los Angeles, and Jerusalem, and children's playgrounds in New York and Tokyo. These peaceful gardens and playgrounds, dotted with Noguchi's work, have helped bring — in the words of one art critic —"20th century sculpture into the realm of everyday life."

In 1985, just three years before his death, Isamu Noguchi opened the Isamu Noguchi Garden Museum in a former factory in Long Island City, New York. Today, this unusual museum houses 200 examples of Noguchi's work, representing all the important influences on his art. Many of the pieces are carved from the stone of Japan's Shikoku Island, where Noguchi spent part of each year. Others are made from clay, wood, or stone, which Isamu Noguchi believed contained all the energies of nature.

On Isamu Noguchi's application for a Guggenheim Fellowship in 1926, he wrote: "It is my desire to view nature through nature's eyes, and to ignore man as an object for special veneration. There must be unthought of heights of beauty to which sculpture may be raised by this reversal of attitude." Without a doubt, Isamu Noguchi has raised sculpture to unthought of heights of beauty. Now others can think these thoughts and go beyond.

James Wong Howe
Cinematographer
1899–1976

"**G**ood with his fists" is how schoolmates described James Wong. So good, in fact, that when, after a few too many fights, he was asked to leave school, he chose to become a boxer. Even when he went from boxing to working as a Hollywood cameraman, Wong Howe compared the similarities of his two careers to boxing. He explained: "You've got to duck, You've got to move fast. You've got to use your noodle."

Born in Kwangtun, China, in 1899, just before the turn of the century, James moved with his father to Pasco, Washington, before he could walk. As his father worked hard to become a successful businessman, James struggled to survive as the only Chinese boy at his American school. Trying desperately to be all-American, he became particularly upset by anti-Chinese behavior toward him, although, as he remembered it, most of his classmates didn't like him any better than he liked them.

After leaving school to become a boxer, James gained attention as the only Chinese fighter in the United States. He traveled throughout the Northwest and down the Pacific Coast to California. One day, in Los Angeles, he came upon the filming of a Mack Sennett comedy in a city park. Fascinated by the creative art of photography, James decided soon afterward to quit boxing and try to get into the fast-growing and competitive motion picture industry.

A fellow boxer-turned-cameraman helped James find a job as a go-fer with the Cecil B. DeMille studio. As a go-fer, James ran errands and did odd jobs. He soon realized that if he wanted to work behind a camera he would have to acquire skills in commercial photography. The first thing he did was to buy a camera and begin experimenting with the technology and art of photography. Then he photographed every actress and actor he met. Within a few years his reputation as a photographer had grown.

Howe's career moved slowly at first, largely because of racial discrimination. As he recalled, he "was supposed to stick in the background and accept a certain number of insults." Then too, he had to make do with the worst equipment. In spite of these disadvantages, however, Howe managed to perform wonders with his lenses and was eventually given a studio contract.

He worked with great sucess on movie after movie, making just a slight midcourse correction as he adjusted to the change from silent pictures to talkies. He worked with such major stars of early sound motion pictures as Marlene Dietrich, Gloria Swanson, and Joan Crawford. Actresses seemed to favor him because of his ability to make them look extraordinarily beautiful on screen.

By the 1940s, Howe was the best paid cameraman in Hollywood and considered one of the greatest in the world. Film offers came one after another. Eventually, Academy Award nominations came, too. Although he was nominated for an Oscar sixteen times, Howe won only twice — for *The Rose Tattoo* in 1956 and for *Hud* in 1963.

James Howe was chief cameraman or director of photography on 119 feature films. Some of his more famous movies were *The Charge of the Light Brigade* (1936), *Yankee Doodle Dandy* (1942), *Casablanca* (1943), *Come Back, Little Sheba* (1952), and *The Old Man and the Sea* (1958).

Although James Howe could not become a U. S. citizen until 1952, when the passage of the McCarran-Walter Act opened citizenship to all foreign-born immigrants, he considered himself more American than Chinese. Having been raised in the United States and having spent his entire professional career in the production of American films, James Howe had developed into one of the greatest American cinematographers of all time.

James Howe shooting on location

Dalip Singh Saund
Member, U.S. House of Representatives
1899–1973

D. S. Saund set his sights high and then reached even higher. As a graduate student in India, he rejected offers to join that country's tradition-bound civil service. He wished, instead, to follow the ideals of Abraham Lincoln and Woodrow Wilson so he moved to the United States. Once there, his goal was nothing less than becoming "a living example of American democracy in practice."

Born into a wealthy family in northern India's Punjab State in 1899, Dalip Singh Saund was taught by his parents to respect learning. After having experienced the limitations illiteracy had placed upon their own lives, the Saunds wanted their children to have the schooling they never had. They enrolled Dalip in school at an early age and watched him advance to a local college and then to the University of the Punjab.

After rejecting offers for government work, Dalip Saund emigrated to the United States where he continued his studies. In 1920 he enrolled in the graduate program in mathematics at the University of California, Berkeley. Two years later he received his M. A. degree, followed by a Ph. D. in 1924. While at Berkeley, Saund decided to join other Asian Indians who were farming in the Imperial Valley.

Within a short time, however, Saund became interested in politics. Unfortunately, according to U. S. immigration law at the time, Asian Indians were denied citizenship, which was a prerequisite for holding political office. Because Saund could not hold political office, he helped organize the Indian Association of America, which sent him to Washington, D.C., to urge an amendment to the anti-Asian immigration laws.

Dalip Singh Saund had always wanted to become an American citizen. As he said in his autobiography, "I had married an American girl, and was the father of three American children. I was making America my home. Thus it was only natural that I felt very uncomfortable not being able to become a citizen of the United States."

When the amendment to the immigration law passed Congress in 1946, Saund immediately applied for citizenship. After his first full year as a citizen, he became a candidate for a judge in the Westmoreland area. To his great frustration, he was again declared ineligible, this time for not having been a citizen long enough!

Finally, in 1955, Saund made his first run for Congress, representing the huge 29th Congressional District of California, which extends from the Los Angeles suburbs to the Mexican border. He set the stakes high, stating that a vote for him would show there was no true prejudice in the United States. He defeated a popular Republican candidate by a few thousand votes.

When he was sworn in, Saund became the first Asian Pacific American elected to Congress. He was appointed to the influential House Foreign Affairs Committee, where he continued to concern himself with Asian (particularly Indian) issues. After completing a well-publicized tour of India and addressing a joint session of India's House of Parliament, he advocated increasing cultural and educational exchanges between the two countries.

Saund was reelected twice. During his third campaign for reelection in 1962, he was crippled by a stroke. Although he continued to campaign from his hospital bed, he lost reelection. An invalid for the remainder of his life, D. S. Saund died at his home in Hollywood, California, in 1973. He had accomplished the goal he had set for himself before coming to the United States — to be "a living example of American democracy in practice."

Younghill Kang

Writer

1903–1973

Three years before the Immigration Act of 1924 closed the door on new arrivals to the United States from Asia, eighteen-year-old Younghill Kang made his way to the United States from Korea. Considered a dangerous revolutionary by the Japanese, who were occupying the Korean peninsula at the time, Kang was truly fleeing for his life. He had arrived in the new country with $4.00 in his pocket and a letter of introduction to the Young Men's Christian Association (YMCA).

Kang's knowledge of English was slight, but as a quick learner he was soon able to write professionally in the new language. He moved to New York City where he earned a living by writing and doing odd jobs. Later he moved to Boston. He worked his way through Boston University and then through Harvard, where he received a Ph. D.

After graduation, Kang accepted a job teaching English composition at New York University. On the side he wrote autobiographical novels based on his life in Korea and the United States. *The Grass Roof*, written in 1931, is set in Korea before 1920. The main character is named Chungpa Han, who, like Younghill Kang, is a young aristocrat fleeing Korea for political reasons. In Kang's second book, *East Goes West*, written in 1937, the main character tries desperately to make a life for himself in America. Knowing he cannot return to Korea, he learns to adjust to the frightening and exhilarating experiences of American life.

While teaching at New York University, Younghill Kang met fellow writer Thomas Wolfe and the two became close friends. Wolfe introduced Kang to his editor, the legendary Maxwell Perkins, who agreed to publish Kang's novels.

The opportunity was instrumental in Kang's success as a novelist and literary critic. Later he wrote reviews for many publications including the *New York Times*. He lived the last years of his life in Florida, where he died at the age of sixty-nine.

Anna May Wong

Actress

1905–1961

Mr. Wong was always telling Anna May that becoming an actress was not a suitable career for a proper Chinese daughter. But the headstrong teenager ignored her father. Whenever she could she snuck out of the house to visit casting agents in nearby Hollywood. Her father, who worked as a laundryman in Los Angeles and could barely support his large family, was outraged at Anna May's gumption. Despite the family's money woes, Mr. Wong would never agree to Anna's decision to work in such a profession.

Ignoring her father's opposition, Anna May appeared in a silent film called *The Red Lantern* when she was only fourteen years old. Although several small parts followed, the characters Anna May played were always the same: sinister Asian women, called "dragon ladies," with mysterious power over white men. And the ending was always the same: rejection of the Asian women by white men when suitable white women came on the scene. This theme, with its racist overtones, followed Anna May Wong from film to film. Her struggle to find good, respectable roles, continued throughout her long career.

Some of the parts Anna May played should have brought her recognition as a serious actress. In 1925 she starred in *Thief of Bagdhad,* opposite the matinee idol, Douglas Fairbanks. Once again she played an Oriental slave, but this time her beauty and talent caught the attention of movie audiences. Even so, although her lovely complexion and fine features were breathtaking on camera and audiences loved her, Anna May could not break the Hollywood screen image of the Chinese as evil and untrustworthy. She begged for better roles but when none were offered her, she moved to Europe.

In Europe Anna May was treated as a serious actress. She made several films in Germany during the late 1920s and became a popular star, acting opposite such great actors as Sir Laurence Olivier. When talking pictures replaced silent ones, she studied German and French, which she was able to speak fluently in her films.

When Anna May Wong returned to the U. S. in 1930, Fu Manchu movies were the rage. The movie character Dr. Fu Manchu, who was based on a character created by novelist Sax Rohmer, was an evil Chinese doctor plotting to take over Europe and America. The Fu Manchu novels referred to "the yellow menace," and this notion of Asians trying to take over the world fed the prejudices of many Americans. Anna May was not proud of the fact that she accepted parts in such films as *Daughter of the Dragon* (1931) and *Daughter of Fu Manchu,* but she had no other alternative if she wanted to work in Hollywood.

In 1936, when Anna May visited China for the first time, she was publicly criticized for taking such roles. She explained that in Hollywood "good" Chinese parts were played by whites and the evil ones by Asians. The casting of the 1937 film based on the best-selling novel by Pearl S. Buck, *The Good Earth,* was an example of this discriminatory practice.

Only slowly did things begin to change. After the Japanese invaded China in 1937, American movie makers saw the value of portraying the Chinese in a better light. Better movie roles, including the *Daughter of Shanghai,* were finally offered to Anna May Wong. She also worked hard for various Chinese relief organizations and entertained U. S. troops overseas during World War II.

After the war, however, Anna May Wong was forgotten by Hollywood producers. Her lifelong struggle to become a respected film actress failed simply for lack of opportunity. When she died in 1961, she was remembered by *Time* magazine, as a "foremost Hollywood villainess," despite her pioneering efforts to create better roles for Asian American women.

Samuel Ichiye Hayakawa

U. S. Senator, Scholar,
College President

1906–1992

Controversy surrounded S. I. Hayakawa wherever he went. He seemed to thrive on it. From 1941,
when as a young linguistics professor he
published his landmark book, *Language
in Thought and Action,* through his days as president of San Francisco State
University, to his one term in the U. S. Senate, he never worried about what
others thought of him.

S. I. Hayakawa was born in Vancouver, British Columbia, Canada, in
1906, where his father ran an import-export business. In 1930, after his
family had returned to Japan, S. I. headed for Madison, Wisconsin, to pursue a doctoral degree in language arts at the University of Wisconsin. After
graduating in 1935, he accepted a position as professor of semantics (the
study of word meaning and usage) and taught courses first at the University of Wisconsin in Madison and then at the Illinois Institute of Technology
in Chicago.

Hayakawa learned to balance his time between teaching and writing. In
1941 he published his first book called *Language in Thought and Action.* It
was the first book to be written about language for a wide audience and
soon became a national best seller. It offered an explanation as to why and
how people react to words and language and was based in part on studies
of how Nazi leaders used language to manipulate people and gain political
control of Germany in the 1930s.

By the time Hayakawa left Chicago in 1955 for a professorship in language arts at San Francisco State University, his reputation as a lingistics scholar was already well established. For more than ten years he lectured at San Francisco State while finding time to write three more books and to lecture widely.

In 1968, during a critical time at San Francisco State, Hayakawa was named its president. Student demonstrators, upset over the firing of a black instructor, were in the midst of striking to shut down the school. Hayakawa acted quickly to oppose the strike and had more than four hundred protestors arrested. Newspapers carried photographs of him nationwide, wearing his trademark hat (a woolen cap of Scottish origin called a "tam o' shanter") and tearing out wires of the sound system that students were using to express their views.

For some students Hayakawa symbolized parental authority gone mad. Many Asian Americans opposed his tactics and were embarrassed by him. For others, he symbolized what a courageous, no-nonsense leader should be. It was upon these people that he would rely for support in his bid for a seat in the U. S. Senate eight years later.

In 1976 Hayakawa turned his attention to politics as the Republican candidate for the U. S. Senate. He ran against the incumbent, John Tunney, and won in a close race. In the Senate, Hayakawa became one of its most conservative members, opposing affirmative action and busing to achieve racial integration. He favored a Constitutional amendment making English the official language of the United States.

After three years, the Californians who had supported Hayakawa and brought him to the Senate were tired of his laid-back style of leadership. They would not tolerate him falling asleep during Senate proceedings and being characterized as "Sleepin' Sam" by the press. When it came time for him to run for a second term in 1982, many of his conservative supporters abandoned him. As a result, he quickly dropped out of the race.

Returning to his home in Mill Valley, California, Hayakawa continued to campaign against bilingualism (the use of two languages) in his home state. Believing that "the most rapid way to get out of a ghetto is to speak good English," he formed the California English Campaign, which in 1986 succeeded in making English the state's official language.

Samuel Ichiye Hayakawa, scholar, college president, and U. S. Senator, died on February 27, 1992. He will best be remembered for his pioneering work in the field of semantics.

S. I. Hayakawa addressing reporters during student demonstrations at San Francisco State University in 1968

Hiram Fong
U. S. Senator
1907

At age seven, Hiram Fong was already earning a living by selling newspapers, catching fish and crabs, and picking mesquite beans. As one of eleven children of Chinese-born workers on a Hawaiian sugar plantation, Hiram could scarcely hope for more than a life of field work himself. But brains and ambition combined to help this boy out of the slums of Kalihi, Hawaii, and into the halls of the U. S. Capitol in Washington, D.C.

Lum Fong and his wife Chai Ha Lum had been in Hawaii nearly thirty years before their son Hiram was born in 1907. They had both come from China's Kwangtung province as indentured servants. By the time Hiram was born, Lum Fong was earning $12.00 a month. His wife, who worked alongside him in the fields, earned nothing. Their children quickly learned that they, too, must work to help put food on the family's table.

Hiram attended public school near the sugar plantation. He did very well and went on to be accepted at the University of Hawaii. Lack of money, however, forced him to delay going to college. He worked for three years as a clerk at the Pearl Harbor Naval Shipyard until he had saved enough money for tuition. Once he was finally enrolled at the university, he completed four years of classwork in three, graduating with highest honors. But there was time also for more than academics. Hiram was an active member of the volleyball, debate, and rifle teams and served as editor of the student newspaper. He also held a part-time job to earn money for law school, and in 1932, entered Harvard University.

In 1935 Hiram returned home to Honolulu from Cambridge, Massachusetts, with a Harvard degree and ten cents in his pocket. He began practicing law, eventually founding Honolulu's first multiracial law firm of Fong, Miho, Choy & Robinson (Chinese, Japanese, Korean, and American partners). Hiram Fong's law practice prospered and his own financial investments became so lucrative that within a few years he became a millionaire.

Financial security freed Fong to follow his political interests. He was first elected to the legislature of the Territory of Hawaii in 1938 and served for fourteen years. In 1942 he became vice-speaker of the House of Representatives and later Speaker of the House. In 1950 he became vice-president of

the Territorial Constitutional Convention, and in that position helped bring statehood to Hawaii in 1959.

When Hawaiians voted on June 27, 1959, to bring statehood to the islands, they also voted in a primary election for seats in the U. S. Congress. Hiram Fong ran unopposed as a Republican candidate for the U. S. Senate. During the elections for state representatives at the end of July, four men were chosen to go to Washington. By winning a coin toss, Hiram Fong became the new state's senior U. S. Senator.

Considered by many to be one of Hawaii's most popular elected officials, Hiram Fong was overwhelmingly reelected to the Senate in 1964. He retired from the Senate in 1977 and has since lived in Honolulu with his wife of more than fifty years.

Sirdar Jagjit Singh

Merchant, Political Activist

1897–1976

The English author Rudyard Kipling often said that the Indians and people of English descent could never really understand each other. Sirdar Jagjit Singh, known as J. J., seemed born to defy that unwritten law. He spent his whole life celebrating both his native India and the United States, while at the same time trying to help both countries understand and appreciate one another.

Born in Rawalpindi, in the Punjab Province (today part of Pakistan) in 1897, Sirdar was the first-born son of a prominent Sikh family. He was named *Sirdar*, a common title of honor for the first-born son and *Jagjit*, which means "Conqueror of the World."

As a child in British-controlled India, J. J. Singh remembers traveling with his father, who acted as provincial judge. Wherever they went they were accompanied by a servant wearing a red uniform. When others saw the servant, they would bow to the judge and his son, thinking that they were very important people. Later, when J. J. was an adult and living in a free society, he reflected on this time. He concluded that the British purposely created such divisions among Indians so the country could be better controlled.

When Singh entered college, he rebelled against the British occupation of India and became a member of the All-India Congress Committee. Following a government crackdown of political activists in 1923, he moved to England where he intended to enter law school. After experiencing financial success in selling Indian silks and cloth, however, he decided to put off political ambitions for awhile.

Singh eventually moved to New York City, where he opened a shop called India Arts and Crafts. By the late 1930s, he had become both wealthy and socially popular. But he did not forget his country or the political cause that was his passion as a youth. As his business thrived, he gave more and more of his time and money to the India League of America, which was established by a group of concerned Indian community leaders.

J. J. took the floundering India League and with his remarkable flair for public relations, made it something that Americans — particularly influential ones — couldn't help but notice. The League became active in lobbying Congress to lift the Asian exclusion laws. At Singh's insistence two Congress members, Clare Boothe Luce of Connecticut and Emmanuel Cellar of New York, introduced pro-Indian legislation into Congress. As a result, President Franklin D. Roosevelt signed an anti-quota bill into law in 1945.

Many said, however, that true respect for India would only come when the country was independent from Britain. To that end, the India League worked with newspapermen such as William Randolph Hearst to keep news of India's struggle in the public's thoughts. Hearst wrote in an editorial that America had a "duty to herself and the cause of democracy to make the British yield." Unfortunately, independence from Britain didn't come until 1947, after years of bloody civil war.

In 1951 J. J., a confirmed bachelor who had always enjoyed New York's varied nightlife, married the daughter of an Indian official in the United States. The two then returned to India, where J. J. Singh died in 1976.

Toshio Mori
Writer
1910–1980

E ven though Toshio Mori played baseball well enough to try out with the Chicago Cubs, there was never any doubt that his dream of becoming a writer took first place in his life. Born in California in 1910, Toshio became Americanized at an early age. Although he had only a high school education, he continued learning on his own. Frequenting libraries and book stores, he saturated his mind with literature and ideas whenever he could. Although he worked twelve hours a day in the family-owned plant nursery and flower shop in Rural San Leandro, California, Toshio disciplined himself to write for four hours each night because he wanted to become a writer. For twenty years he worked so hard he thought his weariness would make him "fall by the wayside." But his determination paid off.

In 1938, six years after starting full-time work at the nursery, Mori's first fictional story about Japanese America was published. By 1941 his stories were being printed in six national literary journals and had caught the attention of the well-known writer William Saroyan, who considered Mori "a natural born writer" and "the first real Japanese-American writer."

At the close of 1941, a collection of his short stories was scheduled to go to press. The Japanese attack of the American naval base in Hawaii on December 7, however, halted the printing of the book and it was not published until eight years later under the title *Yokohama, California*. The stories, which depict the lives of Japanese Americans in California, are written from the heart.

After the bombing of Pearl Harbor, Toshio Mori and his family were among thousands of other Japanese Americans to be removed from their homes and sent to live in concentration-like camps for the remainder of World War II. Hopeful that his writing career would become successful one day, Mori kept writing during his internment at the Topaz internment camp in Utah.

When the war ended and he returned to his family's home in San Leandro, he intended to recover more than two hundred of the stories he had hurriedly stored in a barn when the government imprisoned his family several years before. But the stories had been destroyed by bookworms. Mori's career never quite recovered from this setback, and for the next thirty years his work remained unrecognized.

In the late 1970s, a new generation of Japanese Americans briefly discoverd the value of Toshio Mori's stories and new attention was given to his work. They considered his fiction a humorous, yet respectful look at the lives of the Issei of the early twentieth century. For his contribution to the Japanese American community, Mori was honored at Asian American Writer's conferences in Oakland, Seattle, and Honolulu. In 1979 the UCLA Asian American Studies Center published an anthology of his work called *The Chauvinist and Other Stories.*

During his long career, Mori wrote hundreds of short stories and six novels, the vast majority of which have yet to be published. It is unfortunate that, because of discrimination, his writing has not been taken seriously by the literary community. According to Saroyan, Toshio Mori was probably "one of the most important new writers in the country at the moment [1949]."

Chang-Ho Ahn
Social Activist
1878–1938
Philip Ahn
Film and Television Actor
1911–1978

Through the efforts of Chang-Ho Ahn, Korean Americans could study wherever they wanted and aspire to the highest career goals. It may have been a bit disappointing, therefore, when his own son, Philip, after graduating from the University of Southern California, chose to become a movie actor — a career not considered a proper choice for educated Koreans.

Chang-Ho Ahn was born in Kangso City, Korea, in 1878. There were few opportunities for bright young Koreans at the time, so, encouraged by American missionaries, Chang-Ho came to study in California in 1903. He decided to postpone his graduate studies, however, after seeing firsthand the effects of racial discrimination on the Koreans living in the San Francisco Bay Area. Thereafter the sensitive young man devoted himself to improving the lives of his fellow countrymen, many of whom longed to return to a freer, more prosperous Korea.

Ahn joined a select group of Korean activists in America — one of whom was Syngman Rhee who became the President of the Republic of Korea in 1948. Ahn organized the first Korean community organization, called the Friendship Society, and the first Korean political organization, called the Mutual Assistance Society. The latter merged in 1909 with other groups to become the Korean National Association.

When Japan annexed Korea in 1910, factions within the Korean American community could not agree on the best way to achieve Korea's independence. Chang-Ho believed that Korea must first achieve spiritual rebirth. To this end, he made the heartwrenching decision in the 1930s to leave his wife and children in California and return to Korea. He was later captured by the Japanese and sent to prison, where, after being tortured, he died on March 10, 1938.

Philip Ahn, born in Los Angeles in 1911, one year after Korea fell under the yoke of Japan, never knew his father well. To the young boy, his father was a stern but loving man whose lofty reputation cast a shadow on the rest of the family. When Chang-Ho disapproved of Philip's dream to become an actor, Philip said that he could never hope to match his great father's expectations.

With Chang-Ho gone for much of Philip's childhood, the presence of Hollywood's growing film industry influenced him more than his father's political work. Philip finished college, as his father had wished, but became involved in acting as soon as classes were over.

In his lifetime, Philip Ahn appeared in more than three hundred films, playing a range of Asian characters. His thirty-year career included roles in some of Hollywood's best-known pictures. From *The General Died at Dawn*, made in 1936, to *The Good Earth*, *Love Is a Many Splendored Thing*, and *Battle Hymn*, the versatile actor made his mark on American movies.

In many ways Philip Ahn's Hollywood career mirrored that of other Asian American actors of the time. He, like Anna May Wong, was often criticized for accepting roles that showed Asians in a negative light. He portrayed Japanese and Chinese villains in many war pictures from the 1940s and 1950s. He appeared opposite the all-American hero John Wayne in *Halls of Montezuma*, *Battle Zone*, and *Battle Hymn*. His response to criticism about these roles was the same as Ms. Wong's. "There is no choice," he would say. "I either take these parts or stop acting altogether."

The Hollywood Chamber of Commerce recognized Philip Ahn's contributions to moviemaking by inscribing his name in their well-known "Walk of Fame." He became the first Asian actor so honored. He also became well known for his starring role in the television series "Kung Fu," in which he portrayed a teacher in a Chinese monastery preparing young students to master the wisdom and movements of kung fu.

As Philip Ahn grew older, he thought more and more about his father's legacy. He read and studied all he could about the days before Korea's independence in 1945. At the time of his death in 1978, he was preparing to travel to Seoul, Korea, to honor the memory of his father, Chang-Ho Ahn, the renowned spiritual and intellectual leader of the early Korean American community.

Philip Ahn in the movie Chinese Sky, *1945*

Dong Kingman
Artist
1911

American culture and Oriental technique come together on the canvases of master water-colorist, Dong Kingman — best described by the following excerpt from a 1951 *Life* magazine article: "Trolley cars, signposts, pigeons and skyscrapers tumbled into his paintings in bright profusion — humdrum city streets were transformed into colorful scenes as festive as firecracker celebrations on Chinese New Year's."

Dong Kingman was born in Oakland, California, in 1911. His father, who worked hard as a laundryman, gave up his struggle to earn a living in America and moved his family back to Hong Kong shortly after Dong was born. Dong's mother, Lew Shee, loved to paint and encouraged her son's artistic talent. To attract business to his father's new Hong Kong store, young Dong often made chalk drawings on the sidewalk.

When Dong graduated from school in 1925, he began studying with an art tutor, who taught him both Oriental and Western techniques. Learning both styles helped Dong when, in 1929, he returned to California and enrolled in art school. This was a time of economic depression in the country, and Dong had to struggle just to earn a living. He painted late at night and then, by day, held jobs in a factory and at a restaurant. He also worked as a houseboy for a wealthy San Francisco family. Although much of Dong's time was spent working, he was able to hold his first exhibition of twenty watercolors at the San Francisco Museum of Art in 1929. Two years later, he began receiving $90 a month from the government as part of the Depression-era Works Progress Administration's artist project, which gave him an opportunity to work fulltime.

By the 1940s, Dong Kingman's paintings were exhibited widely in New York. Today Mr. Kingman's paintings are in the collections of the Metropolitan Museum of Art, New York's Whitney Museum, the Art Institute of Chicago, the San Francisco Museum, and others.

A painting made by Dong Kingman on the movie set of a motion picture shows the festive fairground atmosphere that often attends the shooting of a movie on location.

In addition to completing more than fifty paintings a year, Mr. Kingman taught at various universities and art schools. He helped found the Famous Artist's School in Westport, Connecticut, and worked there for many years.

In 1954 he was asked by the U. S. State Department to travel to Asia as a cultural envoy. There, he exhibited his paintings, gave speeches, and held seminars. When his Asian tour was over, the State Department sent the popular artist to Europe and the Middle East. Mr. Kingman painted the final report of his travels on a 40-foot (12 m) rice-paper scroll, which has in time become a treasured piece of artwork itself.

In the 1940s and 1950s, Dong Kingman's paintings appeared in such successful films as *The World of Suzie Wong* and *The Flower Drum Song*. He was widely seen in New York and San Francisco parks, sketching whatever caught his interest.

Today Dong Kingman still paints and plays bridge and chess in his home in New York City.

Bienvenido N. Santos
Writer
1911–1992

"**E**ach time I left the United States for the Philippines, I thought I was going for good," wrote Ben Santos in the preface to his collection of short stories, *The Scent of Apples*. Instead, he kept returning, eventually becoming a U. S. citizen. Over the years, Santos's life took on the shape of the Filipino American experience he depicted so well in his stories. In fact, he once said, "Sometimes I cannot distinguish between these characters and the real persons I have known in America. The years have a way of distorting memories. Now, too, our coming and going appear to have taken the shape of my characters' predicaments. Like those who carry memories as a burden, I find it more and more impossible to travel light."

Bienvenido Nuqui Santos was born in the Philippine capital of Manila in 1911 and grew up in the Tondo, an infamous slum district. At the time, the Philippine Islands were a protectorate of the United States, and Filipino citizens were given the status of United States "nationals." That means that although they had most of the rights and privileges of U. S. citizens, they could not vote in American elections or become citizens.

As a boy growing up in the Philippines, Santos was educated in schools that used American textbooks and followed American customs. He learned the "Star-Spangled Banner" and was taught by American or American-trained teachers.

In 1941 he graduated from the University of the Philippines. Then as a *pensionado*, a scholarship student chosen by the Commonwealth government to study abroad in return for a commitment to public service upon his return, Santos came to the U. S. mainland to study at the University of Illinois, where he eventually received his master's degree.

When the Japanese armies occupied the Philippines soon after the United States entered the Second World War, Santos and many of his fellow countrymen were stranded in the States. They naturally gravitated to the Commonwealth Government in Exile in Washington, D.C., for which some, like Ben, acted as spokesmen for the cause of the Philippines throughout the United States. When Ben Santos returned to the Philippines after World War II, he was "full of stories about his lonely and lost fellow exiles in America." Later, he wrote a collection of short stories called *You Lovely People*, which portrays the lives of these lonely, wandering men.

In 1972 Ferdinand Marcos, President of the Philippine Islands, imposed martial law in the Philippines and temporarily closed schools. Ben Santos, who was in the States at the time, could not return to teach. Instead, he took a position at Wichita State University, where he taught English and became their Distinguished Writer in Residence.

Mr. Santos's published books include *Brother My Brother* (1960), *Villa Magdalena* (1965), and *The Scent of Apples* (1979). Throughout his life, Ben Santos has traveled extensively, balancing a heavy schedule of writing, teaching, and lecturing throughout the United States and the Philippines.

Chien Shiung Wu
Nuclear Physicist
1912

When Chien Shiung Wu first decided to come to the United States to attend graduate school in physics, she planned to enroll at the University of Michigan. But when she found out that five hundred other students from China were enrolled there, she chose another school, the University of California at Berkeley, where the Chinese students were American-born. She wanted to be challenged to learn as much about America and its way of life as she could.

Madame Wu, as the eminent physicist is called by her students and colleagues, was born in Liu Ho, China, in 1912. Her father, a school principal, encouraged his three children to read widely and explore the world around them. Chien Shiung especially loved solving puzzles and, when she entered the National Central University in Shanghai, expected to become a mathematician. But work on X-rays for a senior thesis convinced her that she would like to make physics her life's work.

In the late 1930s and early 1940s, the science of physics was advancing at a dizzying speed. One Berkeley professor, Ernest Lawrence, had just invented a new machine called the cyclotron that could smash atoms. Two German scientists had recently discovered that an atom of uranium split in half released huge amounts of energy. Uranium fission, as this was called, greatly interested Madame Wu, who decided to undertake experiments to discover its possibilities.

In 1939 a fellow Berkeley physicist, Robert Oppenheimer, asked Madame Wu to give a seminar on the subject of fission, which is the splitting of the nucleus of an atom into two parts. During her talk to colleagues, she discussed the possibility of a chain reaction occuring during fission. This would mean that the energy released when one atom split would cause other atoms to split. The continuous series of such fissions would produce a huge explosion. Several years later, Dr. Wu worked on the famous Manhattan Project that was responsible for developing the atomic bomb, which operates on this principle.

In time, Madame Wu began experimenting with a form of radioactivity called beta decay. She stunned her colleagues by obtaining precise measurements of subatomic particles. In fact, her measurements were so exact that she soon gained a reputation for never making a mistake.

In the 1950s two fellow Chinese physicists, Tsung Dao Lee of Columbia University and Chen Ning Yang of Princeton, used some of Madame Wu's experiments to challenge one of the basic laws of physics, the law of conservation of parity. This law states that if you perform an experiment and then repeat it, doing everything the same way but reversing left and right, you will obtain the same results. Physicists were so certain that nature doesn't know left from right that no one ever considered challenging this principle.

Drs. Lee and Yang, however, wrote that under some circumstances this law doesn't apply. Using the experiments of Madame Wu, the two were able to announce to the world in 1957 that their results rejected an established fact of nature. That year, Drs. Lee and Yang were rewarded for their research with the Nobel Prize in physics. Madame Wu was also honored by the National Academy of Sciences as well as several other international science organizations.

In later years, Dr. Wu researched so-called "exotic atoms," using nuclear physics to find the cause of such diseases as sickle-cell anemia. In order to study radioactive substances at very low temperatures and at great depths in the earth, Wu and several colleagues spent long periods at the bottom of a 2,000-foot (610 m) salt mine near Cleveland, Ohio.

In 1982 Madame Wu retired from teaching at Columbia University. Today she continues to lecture and write about the role of women in science and in physics in particular. She also travels the world, collecting awards and honorary doctoral degrees. In 1990 the Chinese Academy of Science named a star for Chien Shiung Wu, the first time they have so honored a living person.

Chien Shiung Wu at work

Minoru Yamasaki
Architect
1912–1986

When twenty-two year old Minoru Yamasaki arrived in New York from his hometown of Seattle, Washington, he had $40 dollars to his name and a few bleak prospects for work. The bustling city seemed at first no place for this slight, shy, second-generation Japanese American. Yamasaki, however, would eventually leave his mark on this dynamic city. In 1973 he would design the twin towers of the World Trade Center that would architecturally dominate Lower Manhattan's skyline.

When Minoru was a teenager, he decided to become an architect. He made his decision soon after seeing drawings of the U. S. Embassy in Tokyo, which his uncle, architect Koken Ito, had designed. Minoru enrolled at the University of Washington in Seattle where he earned a bachelor's degree in architecture in 1934. Thinking there would be less discrimination and racism against Asian Americans in the East and more opportunities for him to advance his career, Minoru left his hometown and headed east. Between the time he left Seattle and arrived in New York City, the United States had entered World War II and Americans of Japanese ancestry living on the west coast had been imprisoned in camps.

After the war, Yamasaki's first professional architecture assignment was with the New York firm of Githens and Keally. While working for the firm, Yamasaki began studying for a graduate degree in art and architecture at New York University. Eventually, he became a part-time instructor at Columbia University in New York.

In 1949 he accepted a position with a large Detroit architecture firm and moved to Michigan where he lived the rest of his life. Early in his career he specialized in large public projects, including the Urban Redevelopment Plan in St. Louis in 1952 and the St. Louis Airport Terminal Building in 1955. The latter design won him the American Institute of Architects first honor award in 1956.

In time, the pressure of undertaking such massive public projects nearly ruined Yamasaki's health. In the late 1950s he was hospitalized for ulcers and high blood pressure. "I realized there's a danger of an architect getting involved in too many things for the sake of society," he wrote, referring to his early years. "He's tempted to forget his real job is beauty."

Yamasaki's later designs reflected his desire to bring serenity, surprise, and grace to his work. "Delight," he told a group of architects in 1959, "must include the play of sun and shadow, a use of texture in materials to give pleasure, and the silhouetting of a building against the sky." His best known designs are the Century Plaza Complex in Los Angeles; the U. S. Consulate in Kobe, Japan; Rainier Square in Seattle; and the World Trade Center Towers in New York, completed in 1973.

The World Trade Center Towers in New York City

Masayuki "Spark" Matsunaga

U. S. Senator

1916–1990

Peace was Senator Masayuki "Spark" Matsunaga's main concern. As soon as he defeated Congresswoman Patsy Mink in 1976 for one of Hawaii's U. S. Senate seats, he became one of the strongest proponents in Washington, D.C., for nuclear arms control. One of the bills he favored most would have created a National Academy of Peace.

Masayuki was born in Kauai, Hawaii, in 1916. He excelled in school. As a young man, he graduated Phi Beta Kappa from the University of Hawaii in 1941 and planned on going to law school. After the Japanese bombing of Pearl Harbor, Hawaii, on December 7, 1941, however, his plans changed dramatically. He postponed his law activities and volunteered for the army.

Matsunaga joined the 100/442nd Regimental Combat Team and, following very difficult training, was sent to Italy to fight against German and Italian forces — Japan's allies in the war. As the regiment bravely fought, their commander remarked, "I am convinced that no wartime commander ever had at his disposal a finer body of fighting men than the l00/442. . . ." For his bravery in action as a member of the 442nd, Lieutenant Colonel Matsunaga received the Purple Heart.

After returning to the United States, Matsunaga won a scholarship to Harvard Law School, where he subsequently enrolled in 1951. After graduating in 1954, he moved back to Hawaii and began serving in the Territorial

Legislature. In 1959 he served in the new state's senate and established himself as one of Hawaii's most popular elected officials. He was elected to the U. S. Senate in 1976.

After arriving in Washington, D.C., in 1977, Senator Matsunaga became known for his support of legislation promoting peace and the environment. He also lobbied for an official apology by the U. S. government for the incarceration of Japanese Americans during World War II. He gave many impassioned speeches on the Senate floor, often invoking the memory of an eldery Issei, who crossed an internment camp fence to retrieve a ball for a grandchild and was shot to death.

Senator Matsunaga's efforts to gain retribution for detention camp survivors were rewarded. In 1988 President Reagan officially apologized to Japanese Americans and issued payment of $20,000 to each of the survivors of the internment camps. Spark Matsunaga served in the U. S. Senate until his death from cancer in 1990 .

I. M. Pei
Architect
1917

As a college student visiting the United States for the first time in the 1930s, I. M. Pei couldn't help but notice that America's urban landscape was very much alive with new art deco skyscrapers. He had no idea that one day he would leave his own imprint on these sprawling modern cities.

Ieoh Ming Pei was born in Canton, China, on April 26, 1917. At the age of ten, I. M. and his family moved to the bustling city of Shanghai where his father managed the Bank of China's main office. A building boom in Shanghai at this time provided I. M. the opportunity to see his first high-rise building.

I. M. was interested in architecture at an early age. By the time he was seventeen, he spoke English well and decided to study architecture in the United States. He traveled there by boat in 1935. After a brief stay at the University of Pennsylvania in Philadelphia, he transferred to the Massachusetts Institute of Technology (MIT). In 1940, at the age of 23, he received his bachelor's degree in architecture and would have returned to China if World War II had not been in progress and Japan had not been occupying China. Following his father's advice, Pei stayed in the United States.

In 1942 he married Eileen Loo and began working for the national defense unit in New Jersey. Pei entered Harvard's Graduate School of Design in 1945. That same year Eileen gave birth to their first son, T'ing

Chung. Later, I. M. and Eileen had two more sons — Chien Chung ("Didi") and Li Chung ("Sandi") — and a daughter, Liane.

Pei received his master's degree in architecture from Harvard in 1946. Once again, the political situation in China made it impossible for him to return home so he joined an architectural firm in New York. By the time the Communists gained control of China in 1949, Pei's stay in the U. S. was quite permanent. Five years later he became an American citizen.

In 1955 I. M. Pei established his own architectural firm in New York City. Calling the company I. M. Pei & Partners of New York, the firm soon began taking on several large urban projects: research centers, housing developments, museums, and office buildings in such cities as New York, Denver, Philadelphia, and Montreal. By the late 1960s, the world had begun to take notice of Pei's bold new approach to architecture. Glass and concrete were two of his favorite building materials. His building designs often included soaring, airy spaces and skylights in vaulted ceilings.

One of Pei's first projects to gain recognition was The National Center for Atmospheric Research, which he had built on a remote mesa in the Rocky Mountains. Others included the huge steel and glass terminal at New York's JFK International Airport, The Everson Museum in Syracuse, New York, and Dallas City Hall.

In 1979 his design of the John F. Kennedy Memorial Library in Boston received rave reviews by both visitors and architectural critics. That same year, Pei received the Gold Medal of the American Institute of Architects, its highest award.

I. M. Pei's grandest and most controversial project was still to come. In 1983 he was chosen by President François Mitterand of France to undertake an extension of the country's greatest national treasure, the Louvre Museum in Paris. Pei's design of a glass pyramid at first seemed to conflict with the grand style of the museum palace that had grown over the course of eight centuries. In fact, when his drawings became public, there was an uproar in France. Many believed this radical new structure would mar the beauty of the world's most famous museum. However, when the first phase of the building was completed in 1989, the public warmly welcomed it. One *New York Times* critic pronounced it "an exquisite object."

I. M. Pei's career seemed to come full circle when, in late 1989, he finished a seventy-story glass office building for the Bank of China in Hong Kong. Because the Hong Kong branch had been founded by his father in 1919, Pei tried to include in his design of the building the two strongest influences on his life — traditional Chinese and modern American. He was deeply saddened though when, in June 1989, the Chinese government's massacre of students at Beijing's Tiananmen Square showed that China was not as open and modern as his design suggests.

Over the years I. M. Pei has received prestigious awards for his achievements, and the beauty of his architecture is admired worldwide. Yet, a greater contribution is yet to be seen. Recently, two of I. M. Pei's children have established the Pei Partnership. Proudly they intend to continue the Pei tradition of changing both the look of architecture and the outlook of architects around the world!

The Louvre Museum in Paris, France

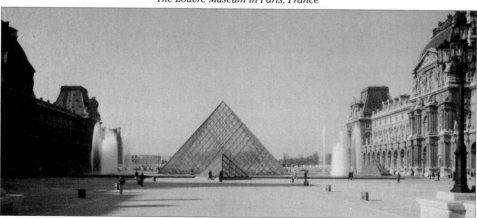

The Bank of China in Hong Kong

An Wang
Computer Wizard
1920–1990

"Confidence," An Wang wrote, "is sometimes rooted in the unpleasant, harsh aspects of life and not in warmth and safety. . . ." For An Wang, this view was reality. While growing up during a time of war and political upheaval in China, An was asked often to take on more responsibilities than other children his age. Yet the harsh aspects of life he experienced seemed only to strengthen his resolve to succeed.

Born in Shanghai, China, on February 7, 1920, An Wang was the oldest of five children. When he was six years old, his family moved to Kun San, a city near Shanghai, where his father taught English in an elementary school. Here, An faced his first difficult test of his ability to succeed under stress. Because the private school where his father taught began with the third grade, An began school as a third-grader. This meant that for the rest of his schooling in China, he would be two years younger than his classmates.

At first, schoolwork was difficult for An. But he soon managed to keep up with the older children. Although An did well in math and science, he had a difficult time with history and geography. Throughout junior high and high school, he continued to excel in math and science but had to take makeup classes for other subjects he failed. He attended one of the best high schools in China. Several of his courses were taught in English and used the same textbooks that American students were using during their first year in college. Although being taught in English made learning very difficult at first, it prepared An Wang for a time when he would be studying in the United States.

In 1936, at the age of sixteen, Wang entered Chiao Tung University where he majored in electrical engineering and specialized in electronic communications. That same year, his mother died in Kun San. For the next few years, life in China became increasingly difficult as Japanese troops invaded China and took over Shanghai. Following graduation in 1940, Wang remained at the university for a year as a teaching assistant in electrical engineering. He then volunteered with eight former classmates to secretly design and build radios and transmitters for Chinese soldiers in Kweilin, China. Although weekly bombing raids interrupted their work, the team of engineers provided a valuable service during the war.

While in Kweilin, Wang received news that his father had died. With both of his parents dead, there was little to keep him in China now that the war was coming to an end. So when he was offered an opportunity to study American technology to rebuild China, he decided to join the two-year program and go to America!

Wang arrived in the United States in 1945. While waiting to be assigned to an American company, he applied to Harvard University's master's degree program. In two semesters, he earned his master's degree in applied physics. Three years later, he had earned a Ph.D in physics. In the spring of 1948, he became a research assistant to Dr. Howard Aiken, a pioneer in computer development in the Harvard Computation Laboratory. Dr. Aiken had designed the Mark I, one of the first computers to operate in the United States. He gave Dr. Wang the job of figuring out how to increase the speed at which a computer could store memory and read it. After much trial and error, Dr. Wang solved the problem by inventing magnetic "memory cores." The core memory system invented by Dr. Wang, and later improved upon by Dr. Forrester, was used in most computers throughout the 1950s and 1960s, until it was replaced by silicon microchips.

In the early 1950s, Wang decided to patent his invention and start his own company — Wang Laboratories — to manufacture and sell his memory devices, which he called Deltamax cores. With only $600 in savings, he rented a tiny office in Boston and went to work. He started with a board of directors that included an attorney and his wife, Lorraine, who he had married in 1949, and one part-time assistant.

By 1952 his work with digital counting devices began to pay off. His memory device had been installed in the scoreboard at New York's Shea Stadium, and for the first time the public became aware of this marvelous tool. In 1955 An and Lorraine Wang became citizens of the United States and Wang Laboratories was incorporated. From then on success seemed to follow success. Dr. Wang sold his patent for core memories to IBM in 1956. In 1964 the company came out with the first electronic scientific desk calculator — the forerunner of the desktop computer.

"People don't want technology, they want solutions to problems" was An Wang's simple philosophy, and it was perfect for the new electronic age. In the 1960s, Wang Labs was the leading producer of electronic calculators; in the 1970s, word processors; and in the 1980s, office automation systems. Because of Wang's engineering genius and corporate vision, Wang Laboratories grew tenfold between 1977 and 1982.

Wang Labs eventually took over a large area of the old mill town of Lowell, Massachusetts, where it employed thousands of people. As the computer industry became more and more competitive, however, problems arose. After being in the lead for years, Wang Laboratories was suddenly overtaken by such established corporate giants as IBM, AT&T, and Hewlett-Packard. In 1986, sensing that his company needed the vision of a younger man, Wang handed the reins to his son, Frederick. But even this move could not cure the ailing company. Frederick resigned as president in 1989. The following year, Dr. An Wang died of throat cancer.

Today Wang Laboratories is reorganizing. Although it may never be what it once was, time and circumstances cannot take away An Wang's extraordinary accomplishments. He surpassed his goal to provide workers with equipment and services to make their jobs easier. Not only did he honor the well-being of his employees and customers but also gave back to his community and society. Dr. Wang funded the Massachusetts General Hospital outpatient clinic and donated computers to New York City's center for the homeless. He funded scholarships and student exchange programs with mainland China. His contributions helped restore Boston's performing arts theater, which was renamed the Wang Center for Performing Arts. He donated to Harvard University and Wellesley College and constructed a fifteen-million-dollar factory in Boston's Chinatown to provide jobs for inner-city people.

Sammy Lee
Doctor, Olympic Diver, Coach
1920

"**W**ork hard in America," Sammy Lee's parents told him, "and you can gain much in life." That's just what their son Sammy did. In 1947 he graduated from medical school. A year later he won the Summer Olympics championship in platform diving in London, England. Four years later in Helsinki, Finland, he became the first person to win back-to-back Olympic gold medals in diving.

Born in Fresno, California, in 1920, Sammy Lee was surrounded by a family who loved him. The outside world, however, wasn't nearly as warm and caring. In the farming communities of California, Korean Americans were victims of cruel racial discrimination. Thinking the Lees were Japanese, many whites taunted them with racial slurs. This was doubly insulting because the Japanese, who were illegally occupying Korea at the time, were enemies of Koreans. But the Lees did not protest the discrimination. Mr. Lee believed that the surest way of fighting back was to change others' false opinions by working hard to prove them wrong.

Sammy Lee followed his father's advice. He set two goals for himself and decided not to let anything stand in the way of achieving them. First, he wanted to become a doctor and then to be the world's best diver. When his friends said that his goals were unobtainable, he responded, "If you think that, you don't know Sammy Lee!"

As World War II raged, Lee graduated from Occidental College and then joined the United States Army Medical Corps in 1942. Following the war, he enrolled at the University of Southern California Medical School, all the while maintaining a rigorous diving schedule. In 1948, a year after graduating, he earned a place on the U. S. Olympic Team.

At the Olympic games in London, England, Sammy Lee achieved one of the two goals he had set for himself. He proved that he was the world's best high diver. (Today "high diving" is called platform diving.) In 1952, after marrying and beginning his medical career, Dr. Sammy Lee achieved his second goal in life — he became a doctor. As if this was not enough, Lee did it again! While competing at the Olympics in Helsinki, Finland, he won a second gold medal, making him the second Asian Pacific American to win two gold medals in Olympic diving competition.

As impressive as his Olympic medals were, Lee's career since then has been just as remarkable. Dr. Lee has managed to combine his two loves — being a respected ear, nose, and throat specialist with coaching promising young divers. In 1956 he was President Dwight Eisenhower's representative at the 1956 Melbourne Olympics, a position he also filled in 1976 and 1988 under different presidential administrations. Then in 1958 he became the first non-white to win the James E. Sullivan award for outstanding achievement in sports.

During the 1970s and 1980s Lee helped guide Greg Louganis to his two stunning Olympic diving victories. In 1984 Lee was an Olympic Flag Bearer and torch runner at the Los Angeles Summer Games. In 1990, he was elected to the U. S. Olympic Hall of Fame, as a genuine symbol of the best Olympic spirit.

True to the beliefs of his father, Sammy Lee worked hard and gained much in life. His achievements proved skeptics wrong and changed the opinions of many prejudiced thinkers.

Jade Snow Wong
Author, Ceramicist
1922

Respect and order were the "key words of life" in San Francisco's Chinatown during the 1920s and 1930s. As a young girl growing up there, these qualities were the basis for all Jade Snow Wong's relationships. Later, they became the theme of her book, *Fifth Chinese Daughter*.

Jade Snow never questioned the authority of her parents, who had emigrated from China to San Francisco at the turn of the century. She always did the proper thing and respected her elders. Respect demanded that she never even call her older brother and sisters by their real names — Blessing from Heaven, Jade Swallow, or Jade Lotus. Instead she was required to say, "Older Brother, would you mind if I...," or "Fourth Older Sister, if it pleases you...." And then she waited for the answers, never interrupting, never challenging.

The Wong Family lived in the back of a small garment factory that Mr. Wong ran. Family life and work were closely linked since the Wong's kitchen and dining room were on the same floor as the factory's sewing room. After Jade Snow's mother prepared the family's breakfast each morning, she would walk down the hall and take her place at a sewing table along with the other employees. Most of the women workers brought their small children with them and often prepared their own meals in the Wong's tiny kitchen.

When Jade Snow was old enough to begin first grade at the nearby American school, her father still continued to tutor her each morning in Chinese history, literature, and calligraphy. When she turned eight, her father enrolled her in classes at a Chinese school as well. So, each day, after she left her American school, Jade Snow would walk through Chinatown to another school, where she learned the proper use of spoken and written Chinese. She would return home after eight in the evening. Jade Snow was proud that her father considered her a bright student. But it made her sad that so many hours in school each day left her no time to play with her younger brother and sister. However, as with every decision made by her parents, Jade Snow's opinion was of no importance.

There were few family luxuries. After long hours of studying and doing household chores all week and Saturday, too, Saturday night Mama took them to the neighborhood movie theatre. Then, when they returned from the movies, the Sunday paper was delivered and they emersed themselves in the comics.

Sunday was a serious time. The family rose early and, after reading a passage from the Chinese Bible, attended a nearby Chinese Christian church. After lunch, Mama and the children set off on a walk together, winding their way through Chinatown's colorful streets. "Next to the Saturday movies," Jade Snow remembered, "these Sunday walks were the best part of the week. . . ."

As Jade Snow neared the end of high school and began to think about college, she questioned more and more the strict discipline imposed on her by her parents. She wanted to attend college but knew that her parents believed higher education was not proper for girls. Realizing that she could not count on her parents to pay her way through college, Jade Snow got a job as a housekeeper for a wealthy American family while she was still in high school. Eventually, she saved up enough money to put herself through junior college.

Two years later, she won a scholarship to Mills College. Being surrounded by privileged American girls made her think about her Chinese upbringing. The more she thought about it, the more she questioned it. Why was I taught to be a good Chinese girl when I live in America? Why was I taught to be silent and obedient, when Americans succeed by thinking for themselves?

Fifth Chinese Daughter, written when Jade Snow Wong was still in her twenties, grapples with these questions. "The new world was full of light and promised independence," Jade Snow wrote, "but the path between the two worlds was . . . a rough one." As a second generation Chinese American, she walked that path, searching for an identity that would allow her to be respected as both Chinese and American.

After the publication of *Fifth Chinese Daughter* in 1945, Jade Snow traveled widely throughout the United States and Asia. Her book became a best seller. Yet, when she returned to her parent's home in San Francisco, they would never mention *Fifth Chinese Daughter.*

Since 1950 Jade Snow Wong has lived quietly in San Francisco working not as a writer but as a ceramicist. She has become a master of this ancient Chinese art, using hand-carved bamboo to decorate her vases. Ceramics, it seems, has helped her to find her own path between the old world and the new as a second-generation Chinese American.

Daniel K. Inouye

U. S. Senator
1924

"**R**espectable poverty," is how Daniel Inouye describes his family's status during his childhood years in Honolulu, Hawaii. Daniel's father, Hyotaro Inouye, and his grandparents had come to the Hawaiian Islands from Japan in the 1880s after a fire had left the entire family destitute. By working on the sugar plantations in Hawaii, Daniel's grandfather had hoped to earn enough money in three years to pay off his family's debts and then return to Japan.

By the time the debts were paid many years later, Hyotaro Inouye had decided to stay in America. In 1923 he met and married Kame Imanaga. About a year later, their son, Daniel, was born. Finances were limited in the Inouye family. To save money, after the other children were born, the children's shoes were bought two sizes too big and stuffed with paper until they grew into them.

Daniel attended both an American public school and a Japanese language school. Determined to become a surgeon someday, he took first aid courses from the Red Cross and diligently read books about medicine on his own. But a series of world events eventually altered his opportunity to achieve this goal.

Daniel was a senior in high school when Pearl Harbor was attacked by the Japanese on December 7, 1941. After graduation, he enrolled in pre-medical courses at the University of Hawaii. But college, at least the first time around, only lasted one year. In 1943, two years after the United States went to war with Japan, Daniel enlisted in the army. He joined the 442nd Regimental Combat Team. After intense training, he was sent to Italy, where Allied forces were fighting Italian and German armies.

Inouye distinguished himself as a platoon leader in Italy's Po Valley. Just before the European war ended, he led an assault on a heavily defended German infantry position. Even though his right arm had been shattered by a grenade and he received other gunshot wounds, he managed to throw a grenade into each of three German machine gun nests, saving the lives of his entire unit. For his bravery, he received the Distinguished Service Cross, the Bronze Star, and the Purple Heart with two oak leaf clusters. Lt. Inouye's arm had to be amputated, and he spent almost two years in an army hospital learning to live with one arm.

Without the use of his right arm, Inouye was unable to pursue a career in medicine. Instead, when he returned to Hawaii, he continued his bachelor's degree in prelaw at the University of Hawaii. After graduating in 1950, Inouye enrolled in George Washington University Law School in Washington, D.C. While in Washington, he volunteered for the Democratic National Committee and was bitten by the political "bug."

When he returned to Hawaii in 1952, he helped build a strong Democratic Party in the territory. When Hawaii became a state in 1959, he became its first member of the U. S. House of Representatives and the first Japanese American to serve in Congress. In 1962 he was elected to serve a six-year term as Senator. Since then, he has been reelected to the Senate each term.

Highlights of Daniel Inouye's thirty-year Senate career include serving on the Senate Watergate committee, which was set up in the early 1970s to investigate charges of illegal activities by officials of President Richard M. Nixon's administration. Inouye's patient but determined questioning impressed national television viewers at the time. He has since chaired other important Senate committees, and in the mid-1980s served on the Senate Select Committee investigating the Iran Contra Affair.

Today Senator Daniel Inouye and his wife of forty years, the former Margaret Shinobu Awamura, divide their busy schedules between Washington, D.C., and Honolulu.

Hawaii's Democratic Congressional Delegation to Washington, D.C.: (left to right) Senators Spark Matsunaga, Daniel Inoye, and Thomas Gill

Anna Chennault
Political Activist
1925

Life in Beijing, China, was sweet for Sheng Mai Chan and her sisters during the early 1930s. Sheng Mai was the oldest, and despite her parents disappointment at having daughters instead of sons, her birthday was always a time of special celebration. She had been born during the season of festivals and always thought Beijing's merrymaking was just for her.

But life was sweet only temporarily. By 1937, Japanese soldiers were positioned on the outskirts of Beijing, waiting for the slightest excuse to attack the city. Sheng Mai's father didn't wait for disaster to strike his family. He moved them from one Chinese city to another before reaching the safety of the British crown colony of Hong Kong. At the age of twelve, the sweet days of Sheng Mai's childhood were over.

A year later, in 1938, Sheng Mai's mother died. The children's father, who had been assigned to the Chinese embassy in Mexico, could not return to Hong Kong, and Anna — she now often used her English name — was left in charge of her five sisters. The girls all entered a Catholic convent school and tried to live quietly, but world events again changed their lives. On December 8, 1941, a day after the Japanese bombed Pearl Harbor, the Japanese attacked Hong Kong.

For a year, Anna and her sisters stayed at the convent school, awaiting permission from the Japanese to leave Hong Kong for safety on the island of Macao. Unfortunately, safety during the war was almost impossible. However, during all the unrest Anna did manage somehow to complete high school and attend Lingnan University.

While still in college, she went to work for China's Central News Agency in Chungking. It was there, as a young, energetic reporter in 1944 that she first met American Major General Claire Lee Chennault. Chennault was a larger-than-life figure in Asia during the war. He was widely credited with shaping the volunteer air force, known as the Flying Tigers, into an ace flying fleet that helped drive the Japanese from China, India, and Burma. "Old leather-face," as this rough soldier from Louisiana was called, was a true war hero.

General Chennault was fifty and Anna nineteen when the two met in 1944. They married on December 21, 1947. Shortly afterward, they founded the Civil Air Transport (CAT), based in Shanghai. This airline flew missions deep into China, dropping supplies to those who who were fighting against a communist takeover of the country. When the Chinese Communists defeated the Nationalists and established the People's Republic of China in 1949, the CAT moved their operation into other areas of Asia that were being threatened by Communism, such as Indochina and Korea. Always strong opponents of Communism, the Chennaults actively worked to undermine its control.

When Anna's husband died in 1958, she and her two daughters moved to Washington, D.C. where Anna became a tireless activist for the Republican Party. Throughout the 1960s and 1970s, she advised Presidents Nixon and Ford in sensitive negotiations involving China and Vietnam. Since then she has supported efforts to overturn Communism in China.

Tsung Dao Lee

1926

Chen Ning Yang

1922

Physicists

Most afternoons, physicists Tsung Dao Lee and Chen Ning Yang would go to their favorite Chinese restaurant near Columbia University campus in New York City. There they would enjoy a multi-course meal and then drink tea throughout the afternoon. Over cup after cup they would talk animately about new ideas in physics. Speaking in Mandarin Chinese, their voices would become very loud, then very soft, and their hands never stopped moving. Many in the restaurant thought the two men were arguing, when, in fact they were simply thinking out loud, exchanging ideas, just as they had been doing since they were both students at the University of Chicago.

It was after one such lunch in May 1956 that Drs. Lee and Yang decided to challenge one of the most basic principles of physics — the conservation of parity law. This law states that elementary particles in nature are always symmetrical. In other words, there is no way of telling which side is left and which is right. Drs. Lee and Yang would prove that under some circumstances this law does not apply. And for their work, they would be awarded the Nobel Prize.

Tsung Dao Lee, the son of a businessman, was born in Shanghai, China. Chen Ning Yang was born in northern China in 1922, but raised and educated in Beijing. His father, a university professor and well-known mathematician, encouraged his son to study the physical sciences.

Lee and Yang first met at the National Southwest Associated University in Kumming, China, where they had both come after Japanese forces invaded their country. In 1945 Chen Ning Yang received a full scholarship to the University of Chicago. A year later, Tsung Dao Lee followed and stayed until 1950 when he received his Ph. D. degree. Dr. Yang left Chicago in 1949 and went to Princeton University's Institute for Advanced Study in New Jersey.

Drs. Lee and Yang were reunited in 1953 when Dr. Lee accepted a position at New York City's Columbia University. There, the two began an intense period of teamwork, exchanging ideas over the phone, in the lab, and, of course, at their favorite Chinese restaurant. Inside the comfortable dining room, they challenged each other with daring new ideas.

When they decided to undertake their test of the conservation of parity law, they chose a fellow Chinese physicist, Dr. Chien Shung Wu, to perform the experiments. Dr. Wu, a Columbia faculty member, often joined the two for lunch.

Six months after the start of Dr. Wu's complicated experiments, she was able to tell Drs. Lee and Yang that her results had proved their theory. They announced their findings to a stunned scientific community early in 1957. On January 15 of that year, the *New York Times* described the news as "the most important development in physics in the past ten years. . . . The fruits of the new discovery may not ripen for another quarter century or more, but scientists are now confident that they are at last on the right road to a better understanding of the forces that govern our universe."

Drs. Lee and Yang were awarded the Nobel Prize for their discovery in 1957. After earning this most distinguished prize in science, the two settled into long, successful academic careers. Dr. Yang continued at Princeton's Institute for Advanced Study until 1965 when he became the director of the Institute for Theoretical Physics at the State University of New York at Stony Brook. Dr. Lee has been the Enrico Fermi Professor of Physics at Columbia University since 1964.

Lee and Yang collaborating on research

Gerard Tsai, Jr.
Financier
1928

"The hottest money manager on Wall Street" and the "complete dealster" are two ways people describe Gerard Tsai, Jr. Attention to the wheelings and dealings of this first-generation Chinese American has been intense ever since he burst onto the scene in the mid-1960s. Today, more than thirty years later, his reputation in the financial world is nothing short of legendary.

Gerry, as he is commonly known, was born to a wealthy Shanghai family in 1928. His father, a textile industrialist, had graduated from the University of Michigan in the United States. Just after World War II, the Tsai family was forced by political events to escape from Shanghai. Gerry was eighteen when he came to Boston and enrolled as a student of economics at Boston University.

After receiving both bachelor's and master's degrees, Tsai went to work for Fidelity Fund, a Boston investment firm. He gained a reputation as a hard worker and began excelling in judging stock deals with amazing accuracy. In fact, he became so successful at managing money that by the mid-1960s, people were watching his movements before making their own decisions about buying and selling stock. News that Gerry Tsai was about to buy or sell a block of stock could force its value either up or down.

Tsai made Wall Street history in February 1966 when, by virtue of his reputation, he convinced 150,000 investors to buy 42 million shares in his new Manhattan Fund. As founder and president of the fund, his assets were valued at $270 million.

Asked at the time how he managed to overcome racial and national prejudice to become the most successful manager on Wall Street, he said "I encountered no barriers. If I can buy [a share of] American Motors for you at $100 and sell it for you at a profit of $50, does it matter if my skin is white or yellow?" Observers point out that his self-confidence is born of hard work and conviction. Gerry Tsai simply does his homework better than anyone else. When he decides to buy or sell large blocks of stock, he knows that, based on all the available information, he's making the right decision.

Shortly after beginning Manhattan Fund, Tsai sold it to CNA, which is a large insurance company. In the process, he virtually took control of the company. Later, after more buying and selling — always perfectly timed — he gained controlling interest in the huge American Can Company.

In 1986, twenty years after the start of the Manhattan Fund, Gerry Tsai pulled off his biggest success yet. As Chief Executive Officer of American Can, he began to sell out parts of that company until, one day, American Can became Primerica, a financial services company. Two years later, the dealmaster sold Primerica for $1.5 billion.

Now in his sixties, many wonder if Gerry Tsai will ever retire and enjoy one of the lovely homes he has built for himself. He has almost left the financial scene before, but lured by the opportunity to make huge profits, he has always returned. Perhaps, as one writer has said, "The hardest task facing Tsai is that he must fill his own shoes and fulfill his own legend."

Patsy Takemoto Mink
Member U. S. House of Representatives
1927

She's been called the most important woman in Hawaiian politics since Queen Liliuokalani. Patsy Mink was first elected to Congress in 1964 and has worked hard for Hawaii ever since, fighting for civil rights and equal opportunity. "What I bring to Congress," she once said, "is a Hawaiian background of tolerance and equality that can contribute a great deal to better understanding between races."

Patsy Takemoto was born in 1927 on the Hawaiian island of Maui. As a little girl, she remembers listening to President Franklin Delano Roosevelt's fireside chats on radio and being very moved by his words. The President's informal talks with the nation showed Patsy that "possibly the highest achievement is to find a place in life that permits one to be of service to his fellow men."

Ms. Takemoto's career in public service began early. She was president of the student body at Maui High School and valedictorian of the senior class. After graduating from the University of Hawaii, Honolulu, in 1948, she enrolled at the University of Chicago Law School. There she met John Mink whom she married in 1951. After Patsy's graduation from the University of Chicago in 1953, the Minks settled in Hawaii.

Patsy Mink went into private law practice in Honolulu. She also began dabbling in politics, first as founder of the Oahu Young Democrats and then as the Hawaiian delegate to the Young Democratic National Convention.

Her first elected position was to the Hawaii House of Representatives in 1957, and then to the Hawaii Senate, first in 1959 and again in 1963, after the territory had become a state.

In 1964 Ms. Mink ran for Congress, the old-fashioned way: her husband John was her volunteer campaign manager and friends and coworkers offered their free services. With only a tiny campaign budget, she easily beat her Republican challenger.

Once in the nation's capital, she wasted no time getting much-needed legislation passed for the construction of schools in U. S. Pacific territories and for education and child-welfare programs. An ardent foe of the Vietnam War, Patsy Mink gave many impassioned speeches on the floor of the House chambers. The war was not only unjust, she told her fellow members, it ate up huge amounts of money that could have been used better for social programs to improve the lives of the neediest Americans.

In 1977 Patsy Mink retired from the House. She and John and their daughter, Gwendolyn, returned to Honolulu. Patsy rejoined her law practice and began to lecture at the University of Hawaii. She seemed content with her quieter life.

In 1990, however, following the death of Senator Spark Matsunaga and a shuffling of Hawaii's Congressional delegation, Patsy Mink accepted a seat in the House of Representatives. She headed to Washington, ready once again to serve Hawaii and its unique multiracial population. Following her reelection in November 1992, Ms. Mink continues her work as a leader on women's issues in general and an advocate of family and medical leave, workplace fairness, and universal health care.

K. W. Lee
Investigative Reporter
1928

"Few ethnic minorities have been so devastated in such a single blow since World War II, singled out for destruction as the newest scapegoat for all the ills — imagined or real — of the murderous inner cities of our country." So spoke K.W. Lee in a speech he delivered October 1992, after receiving a humanitarian award from the City of Los Angeles for mediating between the Korean and African American communities during riots in April 1992.

That K. W. Lee was born to be an investigative reporter has probably never been questioned. No one, however, could have predicted the far-reaching scope and influence of his "beat." From Seoul, Korea, to the West Virginia coal country, and to some of the toughest streets in Los Angeles, K. W. has always been ready to ask the hard questions, listen to the very difficult answers, and, when needed, help fellow members of the human community.

Born in Kaesong, Korea, in 1928, K. W. Lee studied English literature at Korea University in Seoul, before accepting a scholarship to West Virginia University. Shortly after arriving in the United States in 1950, war broke out in his homeland and he, like many of his countrymen, decided that returning to Korea was too dangerous. After earning his bachelor of science degree in journalism from West Virginia, he entered the University of Illinois, where he earned a master's degree in 1955.

The next year he returned to West Virginia to begin his newspaper career. After a short stint with the *Kingsport* (Tennessee) *Times and News*, he accepted a job with West Virginia's *Charleston Gazette*. At the time, Mr. Lee recalled, "the editor of the *Gazette* needed a black reporter. For some reason he chose me."

Being the paper's only minority reporter gave Lee a window to some of the century's most important events. In the late 1950s, he covered the civil rights movement, following Martin Luther King as he traveled throughout the South. K. W. also covered the hard-fought legislative battles that would eventually bring help to victims of the deadly black lung disease in Appalachia. Black lung, a chronic disease caused by inhaling coal dust, afflicted thousands of Appalachian coal miners, leaving them and their families destitute. Laws passed in the early 1960s offered protection and compensation to the miners.

After spending the entire decade of the 1960s at the *Charleston Gazette*, K. W. Lee moved his West Virginia-born wife and children to Sacramento, California, where he was finally able to put his well-honed journalistic skills to work serving the Asian, especially Korean, communities. As he walked the streets of Koreatown, he listened to his ethnic compatriots. Then he did something few other reporters of either race or language had done before: He explained their concerns and needs to a wide English-speaking readership.

For his tireless work, he received numerous journalistic awards, including several for outstanding community service. In 1979, after writing a series of investigative articles detailing the events surrounding the murder conviction of a young Korean immigrant named Chol Soo Lee, K. W. received awards from both the Associated Press's News Executives Council and Columbia University.

In 1979 K. W. became the editor and publisher of the *Koreatown Weekly*. Later he was named the editor of the English edition of the *Korea Times*. His familiarity with California's large cities, plus his dedicated social activism, made him uniquely qualified to mediate between the Korean and African American communities after the 1992 riots in Los Angeles. "It's been a year of our economic Holocaust," he wrote, "Almost every member of my people, nearly a quarter million immigrants in the Southland (of L.A.) have been decimated by this madness and calamity . . . . We look to heaven and ask, 'Why us, why Korean Americans, why Koreatown?'"

K. W.'s faith in new beginnings was strengthened when, later that year, he underwent a successful liver transplant operation. "My new liver," he wrote shortly afterwards, "may have belonged to an African American, or a Latino, or Anglo. What does it matter? We are all entangled in an unbroken human chain of interdependence and mutual survival."

Toshiko Akiyoshi
Jazz Pianist, Composer,
Band Leader
1929

"**A**gainst all odds" could be the tag line for Toshiko Akiyoshi's career in jazz music. Who would have thought a Japanese woman could excel in a uniquely American art form that has its roots deep in Africa? Toshiko herself admits making unlikely choices in her music, but, as she once told an interviewer, she found such deep feeling and certainty in jazz, she could not, not play it.

While living as a child in Manchuria (China) in the 1930s, Toshiko Akiyoshi studied classical piano. She didn't learn about jazz until her family returned to Japan following the war in 1947. Then, this petite, determined young woman became interested in the music that was introduced by American soldiers after World War II. When some American jazz artists visited Japan in the mid-1950s, they recognized Toshiko's talent and convinced her to move to the United States where she could get more exposure.

Toshiko studied at the Berklee School of Music in Boston from 1956 to 1959. She credits Berklee with helping her organize her ideas about music and understand why some compositions work while others don't. After graduating, she hit the club circuit and became a highly regarded pianist, specializing in bebop. She toured with Charles Mingus and Charlie Mariano, whom she married in 1961. The newlyweds moved to Japan, returning only to the United States for club engagements until 1965, when they moved to the New York area.

During the 1960s, Toshiko Akiyoshi grew into a superb jazz instrumentalist, arranger, and teacher. She played at jazz festivals around the world, including the Newport Jazz Festival and Japan's World Jazz Festival. In 1971 she played at New York's Carnegie Hall with Lew Tabackin, now her second husband.

Toshiko Akiyoshi and Lew Tabackin moved to Los Angeles, where they put together a sixteen-piece band, the Akiyoshi-Tabackin Big Band. The Big Band has played to packed houses around the country. Their album *Kogun*, recorded in Japan in 1974, won several prestigious music awards. The band went on to record several more albums and to establish itself as the leading big band in jazz. For many years they have topped *Downbeat* magazine's "Best Band" critics poll.

The Big Band has allowed Toshiko to expand her talents as a composer. She often adds elements of Japanese music to her scores, giving them a striking richness. The best-selling *Kogun*, for example, was inspired by the real life story of a Japanese soldier who was found hiding in a Philippine jungle thirty years after the end of World War II.

Throughout the 1970s and 1980s, Toshiko Akiyoshi continued to expand her talents as a pianist and in 1991 performed a piano concert at Carnegie Hall. In 1984 this bold and tenacious woman was the subject of a documentary film called *Toshiko Akiyoshi: Jazz Is My Native Language*.

Toshiko Akiyoshi's contributions to the world of jazz are unique. As a pianist, composer, arranger, and conductor, she continues to be among the most highly respected in the business. Her big band compositions are standard textbook studies among college jazz students at music schools across the country.

Jose Aruego
Artist, Illustrator
1932

By 4:00 A.M. Jose Aruego is hard at work in the studio of his New York City apartment. While the greys and dirty browns of Manhattan's streets are still cloaked in darkness, the colorful landscape of the Philippines, never far from Mr. Aruego's thoughts, is coming to life on his drafting table.

Jose Espiritu Aruego was born on August 9, 1932, in Manila, the capital of the Philippines. His father, Jose Maminta Aruego, was a prominent attorney and legal scholar. In fact, so many Aruegos were lawyers, it was assumed that Jose, too, would follow in this family tradition.

Jose attended the University of the Philippines and dutifully received his law degree. He passed the bar exam and went to work for a Manila law firm. After three months, however, he realized that he had made a terrible mistake. He didn't want to practice law after all; what he really wanted to do was draw cartoons.

Jose's father, who showed more understanding than Jose ever dreamed possible, offered to send him to art school in Paris. Jose tactfully declined the offer, explaining that New York was the place for a serious illustrator. Instead, in the mid-1950s, Jose enrolled at the Parsons School of Design in New York City.

After graduating from Parsons in 1959, Aruego worked for several New York design studios and advertising agencies. Slowly, he began selling his cartoons to such well-known magazines as *The Saturday Evening Post, Look,* and *The New Yorker.* Eventually, he did well enough to become a full-time freelance cartoonist.

In 1961 Jose Aruego married another artist, Ariane Dewey. A few years later, when their son Juan was born, Aruego turned his attention to illustrating and writing children's books. His first book, *The King and His Friends,* which he dedicated to his son, was rejected by the first publisher to whom it was shown. In 1969, however, it was published by another company. The next book, *Juan and the Asuangs,* also honored his son.

Jose Aruego enjoyed immediate success as a children's book illustrator. *Juan and the Asuangs* was named one of 1970's outstanding picture books. Many other books and awards followed. Today, with more than sixty titles to his credit, Jose Aruego is one of America's most prominent children's book illustrators. Among his favorite books are *Whose Mouse Are You?, Look What I Can Do, Owliver,* and *Leo the Late Bloomer.*

For more than twenty years, Jose Aruego has charmed both children and adults with his humorous stories and animal characters. His images have come from the rich traditions of both his Philippine ancestry and his American experiences.

Mr. Aruego surrounds himself with the lush landscape of the Philippines by filling his apartment with tropical plants and with pictures and artifacts of his native culture. He immerses himself in tales from Philippine folklore, yet, he feels very much an American. Jose doesn't regret his decision to leave behind his law career in Manila and eventually become an American citizen. On the contrary, he feels very lucky. "Lots of my lawyer classmates and professors," he says, "were proud that I made it as an illustrator. I changed professions and changed to what is successful."

Seiji Ozawa
Conductor
1935

As a boy growing up in Japan, Seiji Ozawa's first and only contact with European music was the sweet sound of his mother singing Christian hymns. So when he announced that he wanted to learn to play the piano, his family and teachers were stunned. Why the piano? Why not a traditional Japanese instrument? Despite their disapproval, his parents found a school that would teach him classical piano, in the European style.

Born in Shenyang, China, in 1935, Seiji was the third son in the Ozawa family. In 1944, toward the end of World War II, he and his family moved back to Japan. Seiji and his three brothers studied music at an early age and were exposed to European as well as American musical traditions. Like many musicians, Seiji's talent was apparent very early on. By the age of eighteen, he was well prepared to enter Tokyo's prestigious Toho Gakuen School of Music.

After breaking a finger in a soccer game, Seiji was forced to give up playing piano for several months and switched instead to composing and conducting. From this new experience he learned that he liked conducting music more than playing it and that he was good at it. When he won first prize in both conducting and composing, he decided to become an orchestra leader.

After graduating from the Toho Gakuen School, Seiji followed the advice of his favorite teacher, who thought that he should get his training conducting classical European music with the great orchestras of Europe. Although Seiji spoke only Japanese, he decided to move to Paris to realize his ambitions. In 1959 he persuaded a Japanese motor scooter company to let him promote its scooter by riding one throughout Europe. Then he got passage on a freighter to Italy. Once there, he hopped on his scooter and headed for France. Within a year, he had won first prize at the International Competition of Orchestra Conductors in Besançon.

This prize brought Seiji Ozawa to the attention of some of the best teachers in Europe. He studied one year in Paris and one in Berlin. In 1960 he won a scholarship to play and study in the United States. It was at the Berkshire Music Center in Lenox, Massachusetts, that he was first noticed by the conductor of the New York Philharmonic Orchestra, Leonard Bernstein. Once Seiji Ozawa met the dynamic American maestro, his career began to move very fast. He was offered a job as assistant conductor for the New York Philharmonic and made his debut conducting the Philharmonic at New York City's Carnegie Hall on April 14, 1961.

A year later, Ozawa returned to Japan as a guest conductor with Japan's best-known orchestra, the NHK Symphony. What should have been a triumphant moment for Seiji, however, turned into an unhappy experience when musicians refused to play for him. Many were offended by his "showy" style and felt that he was not showing traditional Japanese respect. A war of words followed that didn't end until a special concert was scheduled by those wishing to mend the wounds. On that occasion Mr. Ozawa brilliantly conducted the Japanese Symphony Orchestra. He has been a popular guest conductor in Japan ever since.

After his Japanese tour, Mr. Ozawa went back to the United States. He was named music director of the Chicago Symphony Orchestra's Ravinia Festival for five summers, from 1964 to 1968. During the winters, he was music director for the Toronto Symphony Orchestra in Canada. He served as music director of the San Francisco Symphony from 1970 to 1976 and was later named the orchestra's music advisor. In 1973 Mr.Ozawa was also named music director of the Boston Symphony Orchestra.

As head of the Boston Symphony Orchestra, a position he has held for nearly twenty years, Seiji Ozawa appears regularly in the great music capitals of the world — Paris, Milan, Berlin, and Salzburg. In Japan he is a role model for up-and-coming musicians; in America and Europe he is admired as one of the Western world's great classical conductors.

Seiji Ozawa admits that, even today, nearly forty years after first beginning his musical study in the West, he is still solidly Japanese in his outlook. Yet, his love for the European musical tradition crosses racial and national barriers. He believes that, "Western music is like the sun. All over the world, the sunset is different, but the beauty is the same." Seiji Ozawa, a true citizen of the world, spreads this beauty as he conducts music throughout the United States, Europe, and Japan.

Seiji Ozawa conducting the Boston Symphony Orchestra

Zubin Mehta
Musical Conductor
1936

The Mehta family knew that their son Zubin was musically gifted, but they were concerned that a music career would lead him nowhere. How wrong they were!

Convinced by his mother to study medicine, Zubin did so halfheartedly until the day he was assigned to dissect a lizard. Then he no longer pretended to like medicine and abruptly left school.

Musical talent was not just a fluke in the Mehta family. Zubin's father, Mehti Mehta, was not only a violinist and conductor himself, but also an active promoter of European classical music in Bombay and all of India. He had founded the Bombay String Quartet and the Bombay Symphony. As a child Zubin remembered being "brainwashed with classical music from the cradle." By the time he was sixteen, he had already conducted a rehearsal of the Bombay Symphony himself.

After two years at medical college, Zubin left for Vienna, Austria, where he enrolled in a prestigious music school. At twenty-one he was awarded a diploma in conducting. Then a year later, in 1958, he entered the Liverpool International Conductor's Competition in England and won first prize. This award gave him a one-year contract to conduct fourteen concerts of the Royal Liverpool Philharmonic, which he did to rave reviews.

By the early 1960s, he was performing as guest conductor for orchestras around the world. At twenty-six he became the youngest music director ever to conduct for the Los Angeles Philharmonic. In 1962 he was named conductor of the Montreal Symphony and became the first person ever to lead two major orchestras at the same time.

Mehta settled in Los Angeles and greatly enjoyed his life in the glittering film capital. Young, handsome, and much sought after by other celebrities, he became something of a matinee idol. All he needed was a star at the top of his illustrious career — a star that was handed to him in 1978.

That year he was chosen by the New York Philharmonic to replace its director, Pierre Boulez. Although Boulez was a hard act to follow, Mehta rose to the occasion. He not only rose, he remained as director for thirteen years — the longest of any Philharmonic director in the twentieth century. By 1990, however, administrative wrangling and bad press caused him to announce his resignation. He gave his farewell concert in May 1991.

That same year, Zubin Mehta returned to his home in Los Angeles and resumed his active lifestyle. Today he continues to jet around the world, landing sometimes in Israel, where he holds a lifetime appointment with the Israel Philharmonic, or in Montreal, Vienna, or New York. Zubin Mehta simply travels, he says, "where there is a need to make music." His family no longer is concerned that a music career leads nowhere. On the contrary, music has led Zubin Mehta everywhere!

Allen Say

Artist, Illustrator, Photographer
1937

In 1984, when a children's book editor telephoned Allen Say and asked him to illustrate a new book called *The Boy of the Three-Year Nap,* the answer was a resounding, "No!" Allen Say was tired of illustrating and wanted to do other things — maybe write a novel. But three year's later, when the editor called again, the reluctant artist said yes.

Allen Say decided that if he was going to illustrate one more children's book, he would at least have fun with it. He locked himself in his studio, took out his old paint box, and began. As he worked, he began reliving many of his childhood memories in Japan and the experiences that led to his becoming an artist. He rediscovered the joy of using his old bamboo brush, a skill he had learned from Noro Shinpet, a great Japanese cartoonist. He discovered, too, that painting was his life's work and that, even at age fifty, he had much more to learn.

Mr. Say credits *The Boy of the Three-Year Nap* with helping him grow as an artist. He modestly hopes that one day he might become very good at painting. If that happens, he says, "I would like to sign my work as my great hero, Hokusai, did. . . . 'Old man crazy about drawing.'"

Born in Yokohama, Japan, in 1937, Allen Say was painting at an early age. When he was twelve, he moved to nearby Tokyo to apprentice with Noro Shinpet. At age sixteen, he moved to California, where he enrolled in the Los Angeles Art Center School. He continued his art studies at the

University of California, Berkeley, and the San Francisco Art Institute, where he broadened his talents by becoming an accomplished photographer.

Books written and illustrated by Allen Say include *Once Under the Cherry Blossom Tree* (1974), *The Feast of Lanterns* (1976), and *The Inn-Keeper's Apprentice* (1979). In addition, he has illustrated such books as *The Lucky Yak* and *Magic and the Night River* by Eve Bunting, as well as *The Boy of the Three-Year Nap* by Dianne Snyder, for which he was awarded the Boston Globe-Horn Book Award for best picture book of 1988. His latest book, *Grandfather's Journey*, is about his grandfather and the rich traditions of his Japanese ancestry. All of Allen Say's illustrations have been widely praised for their movement, energy, and deep colors.

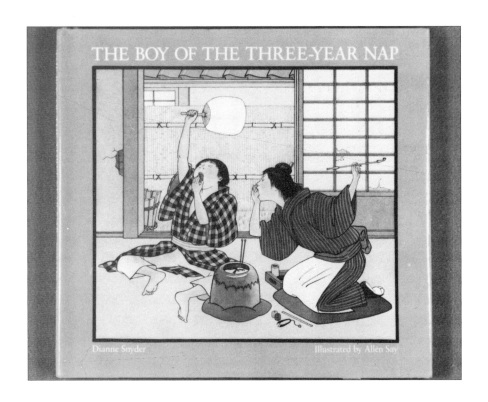

Bette Bao Lord
Writer
1938

I t's no wonder Bette Bao Lord likes to write about life's strange twists and turns — her own has been full of them. She was born in Shanghai, China, in 1938 to Dora and Sandys Bao. Following the end of World War II, the Chinese Nationalist government sent Bette's father, who was an electrical engineer, to the United States to buy equipment for rebuilding war-torn China. A year later, he sent for his wife and children. Bette, then eight years old, accompanied her mother and sister Cathy to Brooklyn, New York, where her father was already working. Because Sansan, the baby of the family, was too little to travel, she was left behind with relatives.

Upon arriving in Brooklyn, Bette wrote: "I docked in Brooklyn on a sleepy Sunday and was enrolled at P.S. 8 in Brooklyn Heights on a sneezy Monday. Dopey and bashful was I because I didn't speak a word of English." And yet, despite a rocky start in her new country, when Bette returned to China in 1985, she was a well-known Chinese American author of books for both adults and children and had mastered English — the language that had once seemed so impossible to learn. She also was the wife of Winston Lord, a prominent American diplomat who had just been named the U. S. ambassador to the People's Republic of China.

When Chinese Communists took over the government of China in 1949, Bette's parents realized that they could not return to China. They moved from New York to New Jersey, where Bette began high school. Following graduation, she enrolled at Tufts University in Boston, Massachusetts, thinking she would become a chemist. She soon realized, however, that her talents lay elsewhere and changed her major to history and political science. At this time she also became interested in dance and embarked on a form of creative expression that she pursued for the next twenty years. Bette continued her education in graduate school at the Fletcher School of Law and Diplomacy, a division of Tufts University. In 1960 she received her master's degree. Two years later, she married Winston Lord, a fellow classmate who was in the U. S. Foreign Service.

In 1962 Ms. Lord was reunited with her sister, Sansan, who had been left in the care of relatives in China sixteen years earlier. The long-awaited reunion launched Bette's literary career. At the suggestion of a publisher, Bette quit her job to write a book describing Sansan's hard life in Communist China and her eventual reunion with her parents and sisters. The book, called *Eighth Moon*, was published in 1964 and has since been translated into fifteen languages.

In the years following the publication of her first book, Bette raised a family and participated as an unofficial member of her husband's diplomatic team. After accompanying Winston to China in 1973, she published her first novel, *Spring Moon*, which was six years in the writing. Writing this saga of a Chinese family over five generations was, as Bette recalled, one of the most difficult things she had ever done. The book was nominated for the prestigious American Book Award and translated into eleven languages.

Her next book — her first one for young readers — was a humorous story of a young Chinese girl growing up in Brooklyn. *The Year of the Boar and Jackie Robinson* introduces us to Shirley Temple Wong, who, very much like Bette Bao herself, sails across the sea with her mother to join her father in New York. It describes the trials of a young Chinese girl struggling to become Americanized. Once again, her book was a great success.

In 1985, after Winston was made U. S. Ambassador to China, the Lords returned to China. Although it was Winston who had taken the oath to represent the United States, Ms. Lord unofficially became his immediate advisor and interpreter until 1989 when they returned to the United States. Just before leaving China, she witnessed first-hand the powerful student democracy movement and its tragic ending in June of 1989 when many were killed at Beijing's Tiananmen Square. Shaken by all she had seen and heard during her four years in her native country, Bette wrote *Legacies: A Chinese Mosaic.* It is about liberation and people caring for people.

Today the Lords live in New York city where they write and lecture. Bette is president of The Freedom Forum, which fosters the exchange of ideas, research, and cultures throughout the world.

Winston, Jr., (left) joins Bette and Winston, Sr. at a ceremony honoring them with the National Committee on U.S. – China Relations Award

Maxine Hong Kingston

Writer, Educator
1940

"I come from the tradition of storytellers," Maxine Hong Kingston once wrote, "and that tradition is thousands of years old; but I'm different from the others in that I write, whereas the rest of them used memory and the moods of the audience. . . ."

Maxine's storytelling tradition came from her mother, Ying Lan Hong who used to tell the legends, myths, and history of the people of Kwangzou (Canton), China, while her family cleaned and pressed clothes in their Stockton, California, laundry. These stories later became the source of Maxine Hong Kingston's writing.

Maxine Hong's parents never thought they would raise their children in a laundry. They considered themselves far more educated than that. Mr. Hong, who was born near the Chinese city of Canton, was a scholar and poet. Mrs. Hong, unlike most women of her time, was studying medicine and midwifery. Yet, circumstances would intervene in their lives and change the direction forever.

In 1924, when Mr. Hong was teaching Chinese literature, he decided to travel to the United States in search of a better life. Encouraged by the optimistic reports of job opportunities, he said good-bye to his wife and moved to New York City, promising to send for her when he was able. For fifteen years, Mr. Hong worked in a New York laundry before he had enough money to send for his wife.

When Mrs. Hong finally arrived, she and her husband settled in Stockton. After working for several years at odd jobs, they were able to buy Stockton's New Port Laundry. The business provided work for Mr. & Mrs. Hong and eventually, for their three sons and three daughters. The Hong's laundry became a gathering place for many Chinese who lived in the community. For Maxine, it was a wonderful time to hear and memorize the amazing stories that were exchanged daily.

When Maxine was enrolled in kindergarten, she knew so little about the language and culture of the United States that she could barely understand the teacher's hand gestures. She remembers that for several years in grade school she didn't say a word. "During the first silent year," she said, "I spoke to no one at school, did not ask before going to the lavatory, and flunked kindergarten. . . . I enjoyed the silence. At first it did not occur to me I was supposed to talk or to pass kindergarten."

A sensitive, generous sixth grade teacher brought Maxine out of her silent world and into a vocal one in which she eventually excelled. Soon she was enjoying the power that came with speaking, writing, and expressing herself in English. When she was fifteen, Maxine won a five-dollar award from *Girl Scout* magazine for an essay she wrote about her experiences as a Chinese American. The essay was called, "I Am an American."

In 1958 Ms. Hong enrolled at the University of California at Berkeley. In 1962, after graduating with a degree in English, she married Earll Kingston. Their son, Joseph, was born in 1963, a year before Maxine went back to school to acquire her teaching credentials. In the late sixties, the Kingstons moved to Hawaii where Maxine began work on her first two books while teaching creative writing.

Her first book, *The Woman Warrior: Memoirs of a Girlhood Among Ghosts,* was published in 1976. It is about the many mysterious, frightening elements of her girlhood — the incomprehensible white people of Stockton; the spirits of her Chinese ancestors; and the powerful women in her mother's talk stories who accepted lives of slavery to their husbands, fathers, and grown sons.

In her next book, *China Men*, she confronts the history of Chinese men in the United States. "Claiming America" is how Ms. Kingston describes her mission in this book. Claiming it, that is, for the Chinese men who worked so hard clearing sugarcane fields in Hawaii or hacking away at the granite faces of the Sierra Nevada to lay the track for the transcontinental railroad. Again, through her writing, Maxine Kingston tries to right the wrongs of the past. In this book, she deals with how American society fought to exclude the Chinese.

Kingston's third book and first novel, *Tripmaster Monkey: His Fake Book*, was published in 1989. She also has written poems, stories, and essays. Her writing remains popular and has been translated worldwide. Above all, it has given readers a better understanding of the contributions of the Chinese to the early development of the United States.

Fred Cordova
Author, Archivist,
Community Leader
1931

Dorothy Cordova
Archivist,
Community Leader
1932

Community leaders, civil rights activists, and recorders of the Filipino American experience, Dorothy and Fred Cordova are second-generation Filipino Americans born in the United States. While raising eight of their own children, they have tirelessly dedicated themselves to improving life for all Filipino Americans.

From 1957 to 1974 they were the leading force behind the Seattle FYA (Filipino Youth Activities) drill team. The Cordovas saw the FYA Drill Team as a way of channeling the energies of young Filipino Americans into activities that would foster self-confidence and pride in their cultural heritage. They also saw it as a way of uniting the diverse regional groups that make up the Filipino American community.

As a result of Dorothy's work with Filipino children and her realization that they had no source to which they could go for information on the history and traditions of the Philippines, Dorothy began the DPAA (Demonstration Project for Asian Americans) in the mid-1970s. "I want my children," she said, "to have a chance to know the history of our people so that they can be proud of who they are." Through DPAA Dorothy launched a nationwide research project called "The Forgotten Asian Americans: Filipinos and Koreans." The project tape-recorded interviews with the pioneers in the Fillipino and Korean American communities. These recordings remain a rich treasure house of material about these early immigrants.

In 1983 Fred wrote a book on the history of Filipinos in the United States. The book was based in large part on information gathered by "The Forgotten Asian Americans" project. When the project ended, Dorothy and Fred established the Filipino American Historical Society. The offices, which house an archive of all the photographs and documents they had collected during their research project and since, now serve as a permanent record of the lives of the no-longer-forgotten Filipino Americans.

Bruce Lee
Martial Artist, Actor
1940–1973

In movie after movie, Bruce Lee kicked and chopped his way through the menacing underworlds of Asia and America. A man of remarkable discipline and skill in martial arts, he not only played the role well but also earned his role as hero for millions of moviegoers of all ages around the world.

Born in San Francisco in 1940, Bruce Lee was the son of Lee Hoi Chuen, a star of the Chinese opera. Bruce was raised in Hong Kong, China, where he became a well-known child actor. At thirteen, he began studying kung fu, which is a type of combat used for self-defense. At eighteen, he returned to the United States to study philosophy at the University of Washington in Seattle. While in college, he opened his own kung fu academy.

In 1964 Bruce Lee traveled to Long Beach, California, to give a demonstration at the International Karate Championship. There he was noticed by the producer of the television series "Batman." Impressed with Lee's skills, the producer offered him the role of Kato in the show. Lee accepted the part and later also appeared in the television series "The Green Hornet," which ran during the late 1960s. Lee soon became disillusioned with Hollywood and the stereotypical roles he was continually being offered. Finally, when he was overlooked for the lead role in the TV series "Kung Fu," and a white actor was chosen instead, Lee returned to Hong Kong where his movie career really took off.

During the 1960s, hundreds of kung fu movies were being made in Hong Kong each year. Most were geared to the so-called Mandarin circuit, which included Hong Kong, Singapore, Indonesia, and Taiwan. The typical kung fu film was short on dialogue and character development but full of action. The films Bruce Lee starred in, however, while loaded with scenes of the fast-kicking, fast-chopping star taking on creepy underworld figures, allowed the star to act. After just a few films, Lee was an international box-office sensation.

Audiences were dazzled by his skills. This, they knew, was not the usual actor pretending to be a martial artist, but a true artist himself. His karate style, which was highly personal and masterful, he called *jeet kune do* (intercepting fist way).

From Fists of Fury, *the first Chinese-made action film to acquaint American audiences with the art of karate/kung fu*

Lee believed karate was part of an inner journey. "It's an art," he once said, "and in learning it you learn about yourself. The punch or kick is not just to knock the other guy over, but to kick at your own ego, your fears. With the ego out of the way, you can express yourself clearly."

Lee was already a huge star in Asia when his movies started to gain popularity in the United States. *Fists of Fury* and *The Iron Hand* are just two that broke box-office records. *Enter the Dragon,* the first kung fu movie made in Hong Kong specifically for an American audience, promised to make Bruce Lee an American superstar. But Lee would never experience the promised fame.

On July 21, 1973, just before the release of *Enter the Dragon,* Bruce Lee suffered a tragic accident and died of a brain aneurysm. He left behind a wife and two children. At his funeral in Hong Kong, thousands of screaming fans tried to break through police barricades to get closer to their fallen hero. His burial was in Seattle, Washington, where today many admirers continue to pay homage to the ageless master.

Dith Pran
Journalist
1942

The story is by now familiar even though its horror is undiminished. In April 1975, the government of Cambodia fell and the U. S.-backed army fled the country. The Communist-led forces of the Khmer Rouge led by Pol Pot, took over this Southeast Asian nation. As the capital city of Phnom Penh lay under seige, *New York Times* correspondent Sydney Schanberg and his assistant Dith Pran, who were covering the story, took refuge in the French Embassy. A few days later, Schanberg was allowed to leave Cambodia; Dith Pran, unable to secure the necessary papers, walked out of the embassy and into the Cambodian countryside.

Dith Pran was born in 1942 in the Siem Reap township near the ruins of the great temple complex of Angkor Wat in Cambodia. He came from a very close-knit family.

From an early age, Dith had a gift for languages. He learned French in high school and taught himself English at home. After graduating from high school, he became a translator for a U. S. military assistance group in Cambodia. Dith had to find a new job in 1965, however, when the Cambodian government asked all U. S. advisors to leave the country. By then, war was raging in neighboring Vietnam, and Cambodian Premier Norodom Sihanouk feared that Americans who were working inside Cambodia might overthrow the government.

For a while, Pran became an interpreter for a British film crew that was working on a film in the area. Later, he became a trilingual receptionist at one of the best-known tourist hotels. But by 1970, Cambodia, too, was at war, and the country's valuable tourist trade had completely stopped. Once again, Pran was out of work.

There were, however, many foreign journalists who had flocked to Phnom Penh to cover the expanding war. Pran and his wife, Ser Moeun, and their three children moved to the capital so Pran could work as a guide and a translator. It was here that Pran met *New York Times* reporter, Sydney Schanberg.

Dith Pran was thirty in 1972 when he first started to work with Sydney Schanberg. By then he already had served as a guide and an interpreter to several *New York Times* reporters. Everyone recommended him. His English and French were excellent, and his understanding of Cambodian culture was invaluable. Pran knew who to see, who to talk to, and how to gain entry into Cambodia's closed circles.

Sydney Schanberg was quickly impressed with Pran's efficiency and thoroughness. The two became trusted friends. In 1973 Schanberg asked the *New York Times* to make Dith Pran a full-time stringer. From then on, Pran worked only for Schanberg, much to the dismay of other reporters who wanted to benefit from his expertise.

Early in 1973, it became clear that Americans were preparing to withdraw completely from both Cambodia and Vietnam, in the belief that a peaceful settlement would develop. Pran and Schanberg covered the story for the next two years until the U. S. Embassy was closed on April 14, 1975 and the last Marine helicopter had evacuated all remaining personnel.

Two days earlier, Pran and Schanberg had said good-bye to Pran's wife and four children. They flew to San Francisco, where they expected to wait for Pran's arrival. Pran and Schanberg were to stay only a few additional days to cover the end of the war. As the situation in Phnom Penh grew increasingly confused, however, and a Communist takeover seemed imminent, Schanberg and Pran — ever the good journalists — drove around the city trying to take its pulse. At one point they were pulled over by Khmer Rouge soldiers who seemed quite prepared to kill them. Pran began talking, however, and talked nonstop until the soldiers decided to let the car drive on. Sydney Schanberg credited Pran's persuasive speech with saving their lives.

The two drove quickly to the safety of the French embassy, which they entered by scaling its tall fence. French officials tried to help Pran, but when they realized the Khmer would kill everyone in the embassy if they believed any Cambodian citizens were inside, they insisted he go. As Dith Pran left the embassy compound, Sydney Schanberg pounded his fists on the cold stone wall, distraught that he was not able to save his friend.

A few days later, Sydney Schanberg returned to the United States, going first to San Francisco to break the news to Pran's wife. Dith Pran's journey of survival, however, had just begun. He first assumed the role of a lowly taxi driver, not letting on that he was an educated man, a fact that could have cost him his life. Eventually, he was taken prisoner and spent most of the next four years in one of Pol Pot's concentration camps, enduring unspeakable horrors.

In late 1978, the Vietnamese communists invaded Cambodia and forced the blood-thirsty Pol Pot out of office. With the Khmer Rouge gone, starving, diseased Cambodians began to emerge from the concentration camps. On October 3, 1979 Pran crossed the border into Thailand and made his way to the United States.

On January 20, 1980 Dith Pran's story appeared in the Sunday *New York Times* Magazine. The article, called "The Death and Life of Dith Pran," described the fall of Cambodia and Sydney Schanberg's search for his friend. It opened the eyes of millions of people to Cambodia's tragedy. It also made Dith Pran a celebrity. He was asked to give lectures, write books, and appear on television. In 1983 he and Sydney Schanberg agreed to allow their story to be made into a movie called *The Killing Fields*. The movie premiered in 1984. The following year it won an Academy award for best picture. Dr. Haing Ngor, who portrayed Dith Pran in the film, won an Oscar for best-supporting actor.

Today Dith Pran is a citizen of the United States and a full staff news photographer for the *New York Times*. He is known for his human interest photographs. In 1989 he returned to Cambodia, to see his surviving sister. His journey was described in an article, "Return to the Killing Fields" in *The New York Times*.

Dith Pran (left), accompanied by Diane Sawyer, ABC news reporter, and Dr. Haing L. Ngor, the actor who portrayed Pran in the 1984 movie, The Killing Fields, *returned to Cambodia to relive his experiences for the ABC Television show "Primetime Live," September, 1989.*

Sydney Schanberg was waiting for Dith Pran as he stepped off the plane at Phnom Penh's Pochentog International Airport. Together they shared memories of that frightening time more than ten years earlier and laid a wreath at a Buddhist temple in honor of the war victims. Before leaving, Pran and Schanberg released two hundred pigeons into the air above Phnom Penh. The pigeons circled the city before flying away. According to Cambodian legend, if you free a captive animal, it will carry a message of peace to the rest of the world. Dith Pran, once a captive and now certainly a legend in his own way, forever carries a message of peace to the world.

Pran speaking at a rally against the Khmer Rouge

Luoth Yin
Social Service Worker, Community Leader
1950

Luoth Yin was a young law student in Phnom Penh, Cambodia, when Communist forces, called the Khmer Rouge, took over the government in 1975. Two years later, he made his way out of Cambodia and came to the United States as a refugee — first to Pennsylvania and then west to Washington state.

His first goals were to learn English and adapt to American culture so he could be of service to the Cambodian refugee community in Seattle, Washington. Since his arrival in the United States, he has achieved these goals and more. Yin has helped establish networks to social services such as counseling, medical aid, and job training, and has returned to Cambodia to establish similar social service networks. In a way he is fulfilling an old dream he wrote about years ago:

> *Oddor Mean Chey sits in the forest*
> *Between garden patch and paddy.*
> *There before you passed on mother,*
> *You taught me this:*
>
> *Study hard, son. Now's the time to build your future.*
> *Once you are educated, once you have learned enough,*
> *You will be able to help our poor village prosper,*
> *Help bring order, bring freedom from oppression.*[11]

In the 1980s, Luoth Yin edited and published the *Khmer News* to help keep recent Cambodian arrivals informed and involved. As more Cambodian children have been born in the United States, Yin's emphasis has gradually expanded to include educating them in Khmer culture. In 1991 he began teaching elementary level Khmer classes at the Cambodian Buddhist Temple, which is the spiritual center of the Cambodian community in Seattle, Washington.

Whatever Yin has accomplished for his family, the people of Cambodia, and the Cambodian American community has been achieved through personal sacrifice and harsh experience. He has had to overcome intolerance both in the United States and Cambodia. Seattle may be his home, but Luoth Yin, like so many refugees who were forced to leave homes they loved, can never forget the love or responsibility they feel for their homeland. After returning for the first time to Cambodia in 1992, Yin wrote:

> *When the motherland first saw me she smiled,*
> *But could not speak.*
> *Full of emotion, I could not speak either, so*
> *I knelt down and kissed her with my tears.*[12]

Luoth Yin continues to work for peace in Cambodia and a better life for Cambodians wherever they live.

A Korean American grocery store in New York City

Korean American Grocery and Convenience Store Business

From the troubled inner cities of New York City, New York, and Los Angeles, California, to the suburbs of Seattle, Washington, and Savannah, Georgia, Korean Americans have taken over small grocery and convenience stores, often inner-city stores that have been abandoned by others. The owners, men like Man Ho Park, and their families, many of them newly-arrived from Korea, work long twelve to fouteen-hour days, combining their profits in order to meet family goals such as adequate housing and good schools, including college for the children.

Man Ho Park arrived in New York from Seoul, South Korea, in 1983. After a sixteen-hour flight, he found his way to his sister's apartment in Brooklyn, slept a few hours, then woke up at 5 A.M. to start work at his brother-in-law's fruit store.

Park worked long hours for two years before he was able to bring his wife to New York from Korea. In 1988, following the lead of previous generations of Korean immigrants, the Parks and their extended family pooled their resources and leased a store in another section of Brooklyn. Their store, Church Fruits, did well at first in the largely African American neighborhood. A few months after the store opened, however, a dispute between another Korean grocer and a black customer led to a boycott of their store and the Family Red Apple store by black neighborhood residents. Suddenly, it seemed that all the Parks had worked for was going to be lost, and they didn't understand why.

Incidents like this frequently occur in the United States. Newcomers (immigrants) with limited knowledge of English and few skills that are salable in the job market, invest everything in marginal businesses, only to be caught up in the middle of ethnic and class tensions that they cannot understand. Before World War II Jewish and central European families ran the businesses that Koreans, Vietnamese, and families from the Middle East are running today in many predominately African American sections of cities. Each group, in turn, has experienced the harsh realities of racism and discrimination.

One reason for discrimination is the misunderstanding that occurs between those who own family businesses and prefer to employ family members and those who believe that local residents should be employed by the businesses they are supporting in their neighborhoods. Such strong differences of opinion often create no-win situations. From the outside it is easy to see that these problems are rooted in the results of a long history of racism in the United States affecting the progress and development of different nationalities and economic groups over the years. Today it is the Korean grocer and the African American customer who are trapped in a pattern not of their making and, perhaps, beyond the understanding of many. Tomorrow it may be someone else.

The proud story of Korean American grocers and what they have accomplished has been overshadowed by the unfortunate violence erupting against them in cities like Brooklyn and Los Angeles. If we look to their children, however, we will see their story in a better light. Through the new generation of Korean American professionals — those who have become teachers, doctors, lawyers, and engineers — we can understand what their contributions to American society mean for their families and for generations to come.

Nam June Paik
Video Artist, Composer
1932

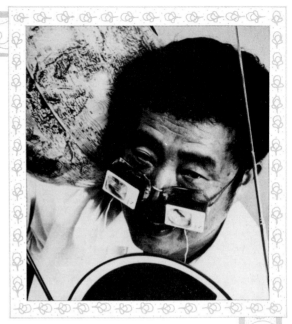

Although Nam June Paik is a serious musical composer and visual artist, he doesn't object if audiences greet his work with laughter. His "action concerts" of the 1960s, where he smashed pianos and poured shampoo on audience members, were either loved or hated.

Paik's compositions have gone from bizarre performance pieces to the world of television technology and video art. He claimed fame as the first person to alter the electromagnetic field of the cathode ray tube (CRT) for art's sake. After years as an avant-garde musician, specializing in electronic music, it wasn't surprising that, given his wit and daring, he would use TV technology to produce art. His contributions have earned him both international acclaim and major exhibits at the world's major museums.

Born in Seoul, Korea, in 1932 he was the youngest of five children. In 1950 the Paik family left war-torn Korea as refugees and went first to Hong Kong and then to Tokyo. Paik hid his interest in music from his parents who believed that such a career was unworthy of their son. When he enrolled at the University of Tokyo to study philosophy, however, he began dabbling in music.

Having decided to continue his studies in philosophy, Paik traveled to Germany where he attended several graduate schools. Slowly, however, he began to devote himself exclusively to music. Encouraged by a teacher in

Cologne, Paik joined a group of experimental composers.

In 1958 he met John Cage, an American composer who was visiting Germany. Paik was thrilled by Cage's theatrical music style. His innovative approach made him look foolish, and audiences would laugh at his performances. Yet it seemed to open up new avenues for music and encouraged Paik to begin experimenting on his own. Soon Paik's action concerts were being billed as hilarious and outrageous. Just as they were becoming more widely accepted, however, Paik switched his attention to video technology.

He began taking apart black-and-white TV sets and hooking them up to microphones in order to watch the sound waves leap across the television screen. Later he reversed the black-and-white controls to make negative images and then interfered with the electromagnetic field to produce bizarre shapes. He held his first video art show in Germany in 1963.

Within a year he had begun experimenting with color sets and invented the concept of "video painting." Accompanied by a robot on his first visit to the United States in 1964, Paik settled in New York City. The first showing of his video painting on home television came in 1968 when a public television station asked him to produce an hour-long special called "The Medium Is the Medium." Another program followed called "Video Commune." This show featured a video synthesizer that Paik had designed and built himself.

For the next twenty-five years, Paik turned video technology into both art and entertainment. In 1982 the Whitney Museum of American Art honored him by featuring sixty of his video installations as well as sculptures and musical scores. The show then traveled to Chicago, San Francisco, Berlin, and Vienna.

A United States citizen since 1976, today Nam June Paik lives in New York City with his Japanese wife, who is also a video artist.

Wendy Lee Gramm
Economist
1945

Wendy Lee grew up in Hawaii in the 1950s, near Waialeale's sugar refinery, where her father and grandfather worked long hours. From an early age, she learned how important hard work and determination were to success — something she would someday value as a Korean American in the business world.

When Wendy won a scholarship to Wellesley College in Massachusetts in the mid-1960s, she used her excellent math skills and interest in business to become an economics major. Graduating in 1966, she moved to Evanston, Illinois, where she began graduate school at Northwestern University. In 1971 she received her Ph.D. from Northwestern. Her thesis was on married women in the labor force, a topic she herself would soon understand well.

During her last year at Northwestern, Wendy Lee traveled around the country looking for a teaching job. One interview took place at Texas A & M University in College Station. There she met fellow economist William Philip Gramm. Within a year, she was not only teaching at Texas A & M, but also married to Dr. Gramm.

For several years, both Gramms taught at Texas A & M. Their two sons were born in 1973 and 1975. In 1976 Phil Gramm decided to enter politics. He ran for one of Texas's U.S. Senate seats and lost. Two years later, however, when he was elected to the U. S. House of Representatives, the Gramm family moved to Washington, D.C.

Wendy Lee Gramm did not waste time regretting losing her teaching position at Texas A & M. Instead, she thought about how she might use her economics training in Washington, D.C. In 1982 she took a job with the Federal Trade Commission, eventually becoming the director of its Bureau of Economics. But two years later, she resigned her position to campaign for her husband's reelection to the U. S. Senate. After his reelection, she became the administrator of the Office of Information and Regulatory Affairs in the Office of Management and Budget (OMB). She served in that office for two years.

In 1987 Ms. Gramm was nominated and approved to become Chair of the Commodity Futures Trading Commission. "This job is fascinating," she recently told an interviewer, "because it is an international marketplace, with the most innovative, cutting-edge financial market issues." She was nominated and approved for a second term in August 1990.

While Wendy and Phil Gramm's commitment to public service leaves little time beyond work hours, they insist on planning several family vacations each year. Their favorite destination is, not surprisingly, Hawaii, where Ms. Gramm insists they immediately take off their shoes and run barefoot on the beach.

Ellison S. Onizuka

Astronaut, Aerospace Engineer

1946–1986

On his first flight into space, Lt. Colonel Ellison S. Onizuka took along a few mementos. The Kona coffee and macadamia nuts were from the Hawaiian village where he was born and raised. The Buddhist medallion was from his father, who had instilled in him the values of patience, hard work, and dedication to duty. Ellison also took along patches from the Japanese American 442nd combat regiment, whose patriotism and courage during World War II were legendary. These same qualities had brought him to this point — to the lift-off of the space shuttle *Discovery* and to the fulfillment of all his dreams.

Ellison Onizuka was born on June 24, 1946, in Keopu, Hawaii. The grandson of Hawaiian plantation workers, Ellison showed an early interest in flying and engineering. In 1964 he won a scholarship to the University of Colorado, where he majored in aerospace engineering and participated in the Air Force ROTC program.

In 1969, just before earning a master of science degree from Colorado, Ellison married fellow Hawaiian Lorna Yoshida. As third-generation Japanese Americans, they were the first in their families to choose their marriage partners. Just before the couple moved to the McClellan Air Force Base in Sacramento, California, their first daughter, Janelle, was born. A second girl, Darien, was born a few years later. At McClellan, Ellison designed flight test programs and aircraft safety systems.

A short time later, Ellison was accepted into the competitive Air Force Test Pilot School at Edwards Air Force Base in California's Mojave Desert. At Edwards he tested aircraft and taught engineering to other pilots. His skills were noticed by Air Force and NASA officials, and he was invited to apply to the astronaut program. In the early 1970s, NASA's focus had moved away from the *Apollo* moon missions to the *Skylab* space shuttles, for which they needed many new specialists.

Of the 8,100 candidates who applied for NASA's space-shuttle program, Ellison was among the first 220 who were interviewed. His all-around qualifications led to his becoming one of the thirty-five men and women chosen for *Skylab*.

The Onizuka family moved to Houston, Texas, in 1978, where Ellison could begin training at the Johnson Space Center. His schedule included classes in computers, astronomy, oceanography, and mathematics. He trained in a weightless atmosphere and practiced simulated lift-offs and landing procedures. Since Ellison was a mission specialist, he also received training from the Department of Defense on various confidential technical assignments.

In 1982 Onizuka was one of five astronauts chosen for the flight of the *Discovery*, which was launched on January 24, 1985. The mission lasted only three days. The rounds of parades and public appearances, however, celebrating the first Asian American in space lasted for months. After the *Discovery* flight, Ellison returned to Hawaii to visit both family and friends and to speak to school children throughout the islands.

By mid-1985 Lt. Colonel Onizuka was back in Houston training for his next mission, the flight of the *Challenger*. Unlike the *Discovery*, the *Challenger* assignment was not top-secret. It was to carry seven men and women of various backgrounds, including a schoolteacher from New Hampshire named Christa McAuliffe. Her highly publicized participation meant that many Americans — especially schoolchildren — would be watching the televised lift-off from Florida's Kennedy Space Center the morning of January 28, 1986.

The fate of the *Challenger* is now a tragic part of American history. Seventy-three seconds after lift-off, a malfunction in the rocket booster caused it to blow up and disappear into the Atlantic Ocean, just off the Florida coast. None of the *Challenger* crew survived.

Although Ellison Onizuka's life was cut short, he left behind an impressive legacy for those who are striving to attain the impossible and create a better world. His dedication and personal goals are best remembered in a message he delivered to a group of high school graduates in Hawaii:

> "Every generation has the obligation to free men's minds for a look at new worlds. . . . to look out from a higher plateau than the last generation. . . . Make your life count — and the world will be a better place because you tried."[13]

Connie Chung
News Anchor and Reporter
1946

When CBS-TV hired Connie Chung to be an on-air reporter in 1972, it seemed as though the network was just filling an ethnic quota. At the time, the Federal Communications Commission (FCC) was pressuring CBS, NBC, and ABC to hire more women and minorities. Connie often joked that by hiring her, CBS had gotten two in one — a woman and a member of an ethnic minority. They also got, as television viewers soon discovered, an insightful reporter.

Constance Yu-hwa Chung was born on August 20, 1946. She was the last of William Ling and Margaret Wa Chung's ten children and the only child to be born in the United States. The Chungs had fled Shanghai, China, in 1944, in the midst of a Japanese bombing raid. By then, World War II already had taken its toll on the family. Five children had died since 1941.

To prevent further harm to his family and secure their future, Connie's father decided to take them to America. In 1945 Mr. & Mrs. Chung and Connie's four sisters arrived in Washington, D.C., where Mr. Chung began working for the Chinese Embassy.

By the time Connie was born, life seemed to have returned to normal. Connie was raised as a typical American girl. In high school, she acted in plays and took part in student government, and then began showing strong interest in politics and world events. In college, she did some speech writing and press releases for a New York congressman.

In 1965, after graduating from the University of Maryland with a degree in journalism, Ms. Chung became a news department secretary at WTTG, a Washington television station. She advanced quickly, becoming a newswriter, then an editor, and finally an on-air reporter. After having caught the interest of CBS's Washington bureau in 1972, Chung was hired as one of their first female reporters.

In 1976 the local CBS affiliate in Los Angeles hired Ms. Chung to be their news anchor. She appeared on the air three times a day and quickly became very popular with viewers. She won numerous awards for broadcasting and became the highest paid local news anchor in the country.

By 1983, however, the year before the next presidential election, Chung was eager to get back into the arena of national politics. After accepting a job offer from NBC to anchor both a morning news show called "NBC at Sunrise"and the Saturday edition of NBC Nightly News, she moved to New York City.

At NBC Ms. Chung also co-anchored NBC's weekly news magazine program with Roger Mudd. Time spent at NBC doing documentaries and informative programs gave her national exposure and boosted her popularity. In March 1989 she rejoined CBS News, where she had first begun her career. Now, in addition to anchoring the "CBS Evening News, Sunday Edition," she hosted her own show, "Saturday Night with Connie Chung." As ratings grew, Ms. Chung's program moved to Monday nights and was renamed "Face to Face with Connie Chung."

Ms. Chung's latest responsibilities include a new prime-time magazine show on CBS called "Eye to Eye with Connie Chung" and a co-anchor position with Dan Rather on "CBS Evening News."

Lawrence Yep
Writer
1948

Born in 1948 on the fringes of San Francisco's Chinatown and a black ghetto, Lawrence Yep knew nothing about white America until he entered high school. And then, surrounded by three very different cultures, he felt cast off by all of them. This sense of alienation explains his early interest in writing science fiction. In science fiction, after all, the creator can start fresh and make up an entirely new culture — something Lawrence Yep wanted to do all along.

After graduating from the University of California at Santa Cruz in 1970, Yep went on to earn a Ph. D. in English from the State University of New York at Buffalo. Soon after finishing college, he published his first book, *Sweetwater*, which tells the story of an early colonist from Earth who visits the star Harmony.

His best known work, *Dragonwings*, is a combination of historical fiction and fantasy. It is set in early twentieth century San Francisco. Based on a true story, it tells the story of a Chinese man named Windrider who fulfills his dream of building and flying an airplane.

Other books by Lawrence Yep include *Child of the Owl, Sea Glass,* and *Dragon of the Lost Sea*, which he dedicated to his grandmother, who played an important part in his career. From the family stories and Chinese fairy tales that she told him, Yep developed a wonderful sense of heritage that permeates his writing.

One of Yep's recent books, *The Star Fisher,* is based on his family's history. The main character, fifteen-year-old Joan Lee, is loosely based on Yep's own mother. Other characters are based on Yep's grandparents, aunts, and uncles, who left their home and laundry business in Ohio in the 1920s and moved to the small, remote city of Clarksburg, West Virginia, to start a new life. There they experienced discrimination from the towns-people and struggled to survive within two very distinct cultures — Chinese and American. Today Lawrence Yep lives in San Francisco, California, and teaches writing at the University of California, Berkeley. Through his writing and storytelling, he continues to focus on Asian America and on what separates one culture — whether real or imaginary — from another.

June Kuramoto
Musician
1948

June Okida Kuramoto first heard the magical sounds of the *koto* (a Japanese musical instrument) when her mother took her to a concert performed by Madame Kazue Kudo in Los Angeles. After that memorable experience, June begged her mother to let her learn how to play the *koto* from Madame Kudo. June's mother finally agreed. Since then, the relationship between June Kuramoto and Madame Kudo has grown into a rich musical partnership.

June Okida Kuramoto was born in Saitama-ken, Japan, in 1948 and moved with her family to Los Angeles five years later. From the age of six, June took *koto* lessons once a week and practiced for at least an hour every day after school. Schoolmates made fun of her interest in the heavy, six-foot-long instrument that made what they called "grandma music." But June was able to ignore their taunts. She studied traditional *koto* music from Madame Kudo, and then went on to get her masters degree from the Michio Miyagi Koto School of Tokyo.

Between high school and college, June began to develop a new style to her music. As if in answer to the jeers about "grandma music," June looked for ways to bring the rich sounds of the koto together with the unique strains of American rock and jazz. In her early twenties, she began working with a jazz flutist named Dan Kuramoto, whom she married in 1971. Together they brought a new dimension to Dan's band called *Hiroshima*.

Besides the flute and *koto*, they eventually added keyboards, woodwinds, drums, bass, and guitar to create a musical style that was distinctly Asian American. Later they included percussion and the Japanese *taiko* drums.

During the 1970s and 1980s, *Hiroshima* recorded six albums and toured often, playing in well-known big-city nightclubs. They received a Grammy nomination in 1981, and their album *Go* was named Best Jazz Album at the Soul Train Music Awards in 1988. It also was on the top of *Billboard's Contemporary Jazz Album* charts for eight weeks that same year.

Today, when not working with *Hiroshima*, Ms. Kuramoto tours and records with other well-known musical artists. Her *koto* music adds a special sound to the music of many contemporary pop and jazz artists. She has performed with Manhattan Transfer, Stanley Clarke, Martika, Foreigner, and Teddy Pendergrass.

In 1989 she and three other members of *Hiroshima* appeared in a play called *Sansei* (third-generation Japanese Americans). Based on their own experiences growing up in Los Angeles, the play was a kind of portrait of Japanese American life in music and drama.

"I see myself as a human being first, then a musician," Ms. Kuramoto once told an interviewer. All her life, her goal has been to move away from the stereotyped view of Asian Americans and focus instead on their rich cultural heritage. Through her music and songs, June Kuramoto is achieving this goal. Although she has been criticized by some people in the Asian community for combining classical *koto* music and western instruments, many strongly support her style and identify with her music.

Wayne Wang
Film Director
1949

In 1949, six days after Mr. & Mrs. Wang had escaped to Hong Kong, China, during the Communist takeover, their son Wayne was born. It was a rocky start by any standards. But Mr. Wang, once a prosperous merchant in his native Tsingtao, had one important advantage. He had learned English while selling merchandise to American sailors at the American naval base near Tsingtao. Later it would prove invaluable when he opened an import-export business.

Although the Wangs prospered in Hong Kong, they were never happy there. They had resigned themselves to the fact that they might never be able to return to their homeland, and looked, instead, toward America for hope.

In 1968 Wayne traveled to America to attend college in California and become "truly American." While in graduate school at California College of Arts and Crafts, he studied film production. But he saw little chance of breaking into the film-making business in the highly competitive Los Angeles area, so he returned to Hong Kong. There he became the director of a popular television series.

Still eager to break into serious film making, he and his wife, Cora Miao, returned to the United States where they immediately began work on a film called *Chan Is Missing*. Wang hoped the film would speak to young Asian Americans who might be just as mixed up as he was about whether to be more "Asian" or more "American."

The low-budget film cost $22,000 to produce and was released in 1983. It won the attention of many critics who acknowledged its gentle humor.

His next film, *Dim Sum*, cost four times as much as his first film. It proved much more difficult to make because Wang could not decide whether he wanted to make a slick, commercially successful film or a quiet story about characters he knew and loved. Halfway through production of the film, he shifted gears and focused on the latter — the relationship between a daughter and her widowed mother.

Dim Sum was completed in May 1985 and shown that same year at the Cannes Film Festival. It confirmed what critics and moviegoers had been saying about Wayne Wang already — that he is a graceful, sensitive artist who portrays Chinese American life in a humorous, yet tender way. One critic says that in Wang's movies there is room both for Confucius and American soap operas.

Since production of *Dim Sum*, Wang has completed other films, including *Eat a Bowl of Tea* (1989) and *Life Is Cheap . . . but Toilet Paper Is Expensive* (1990). Wayne Wang continues to be one of the new voices for young Chinese Americans as he takes the reality of their lives and sensitively portrays it on screen.

A photograph of one of the scenes from Wayne Wang's film, Chan Is Missing

Amy Tan
Novelist
1952

A few years ago, when Amy Tan asked her mother what life had been like in Shanghai, China, during World War II, Dora Tan said simply: "I wasn't affected." When Ms.Tan pressed for more details, her mother began to tell her stories of the frequent Japanese bombing raids that made her frightened family run first to the city's east gate, then to the west gate, to avoid the bombs. "But I thought you said you weren't affected," Ms. Tan said. "I wasn't. . . ." her mother answered. "I wasn't killed."

The difference between the American and Chinese perspectives of war and danger and "being affected" became the subject of Amy Tan's second best-selling novel, *The Kitchen God's Wife,* published in 1991.

Amy's parents came from China to the United States after World War II. They met in San Francisco, where they eventually married and raised three children. Like many Chinese parents raising children in America, the Tans wanted them to take advantage of all the opportunities they had missed. They urged them to study hard and fit into American society. Life seemed to progress in an ordinary manner until Amy's father and brother both died of cancer in 1967. Then Amy's mother told her and her sister something about herself that would change them forever.

Before coming to America, Mrs. Tan had been married and divorced. When she had fled Shanghai, China, after World War II, she had left behind three daughters. She had planned to bring them to the United States once she was settled, but when the Communists took over China in 1949, the girls were not allowed to leave. Then when communication between the citizens of China and the U. S. was forbidden, she lost track of her children. For Amy Tan, this news changed everything. Now she was deeply tied to China in ways she had never thought possible.

In 1987 Mrs. Tan and her daughters were reunited in China. The joyous occasion proved to Amy that her ties to her lost sisters and to China were much stronger than she had ever imagined. How strongly she was affected by the new relationship in her life is evident in the book she published two years later.

The Joy Luck Club, which reflects Ms. Tan's own experiences, is about four first-generation Chinese mothers and their "Americanized" second-generation daughters. The mothers, who meet often to drink tea and play a Chinese game called *mah-jong*, talk about their Chinese pasts and their American children who seem more like strangers to them than kin. The daughters are embarrassed by their mothers who, they believe, wear "funny Chinese dresses with stiff stand-up collars and blooming branches of embroidered silk. . . ." The misunderstandings continue until one of the club members dies and her daughter takes her place in *The Joy Luck Club*. Then the daughter begins to appreciate her rich Chinese heritage. She comes to understand the pain suffered by the older women and the changes they have had to make in their personal lives.

Today Amy Tan lives with her husband in San Francisco. She continues to reflect on her Chinese heritage and write about its significance to her as an American.

Myung-Whun Chung
Musician, Music Director, Conductor
1953

Controversy swirled around the opening of the new Opera de la Bastille in Paris, France. For months, even years, before its scheduled first performance in the summer of 1989 nothing seemed to go right. The building — modern and glassy on one of Paris's most historic sites — cost more than $400 million, yet few found anything about it to praise.

About a year before the opening of the Opera de la Bastille, the project's top administrator was fired. His replacement then fired the conductor who had been chosen to head the opera company. Then, in yet another risky move, the new conductor hired to lead the company into its most important season was a thirty-seven-year old Korean-born American named Myung-Whun Chung.

Myung-Whun Chung could not speak French and did not have much experience conducting opera. He was a highly esteemed pianist and orchestral conductor, who had proven he could rise to tough challenges. But was he, the French public wondered, a miracle worker?

Myung-Whun Chung was born in Seoul, Korea, on January 22, 1953, the sixth of seven children of musically gifted parents. Music was so important to the Chungs that when, in the early 1950s, they had to flee the invading Communist-led forces of North Korea, their piano was one of the only family treasures they brought with them during the escape.

At the age of seven, Myung-Whun made his piano debut with the Seoul Philharmonic. He wasn't terribly nervous, though, because three of his sisters had played with the Seoul Philharmonic before him. Myung-Wha had played the cello, Kyung-Wha the violin, and Myung-So the flute.

When Myung-Whun's sister, Kyung-Wha, won a scholarship to New York City's famed Juilliard School, the entire family moved to the United States. In 1961 the Chungs settled in Seattle, Washington. Kyung-Wha and Myung-Wha attended the Julliard in New York while Myung-Whun completed high school. Then, he, too, moved to New York City to attend Juilliard. At Juilliard, Myung-Whun's focus shifted from piano playing to conducting. After graduation, however, he still wasn't sure whether his future lay with the piano or the conductor's baton.

During his years in New York, Myung-Whun Chung became a U. S. citizen and met Sunyol, the woman he later married. In 1978 he was named Assistant Conductor of the Los Angeles Symphony and within a few years became an Associate Conductor. He grew weary, though, of the additional duties of a music director, such as fund raising and publicity. By the early 1980s, he was ready for a change. He and his wife moved to Europe so that he could conduct in different cities of the world.

Chung became the music director and prinicpal conductor for the Radio Symphony Orchestra in Saarbrücken, West Germany in 1984. A few years later, he and Sunyol moved to Italy where he performed as a principal guest conductor. He also appeared with major orchestras in France, Britain, Israel, Germany, the Netherlands, and the United States.

By 1989, when Chung became the music director of the Opera de la Bastille, his life had changed greatly from his carefree days in New York and Los Angeles. He and his wife were now the parents of three sons, and he was an experienced conductor and director. They welcomed the opportunity to live and work in Paris. Despite the Bastille Opera's problems, the Chungs were looking forward to Myung-Whun's new position.

Almost immediately, Chung was thrown into the middle of enormous problems. The Opera de la Bastille, whose construction was announced by French President François Mitterand in 1982, was to open in time for the 200th anniversary celebration of the start of the French Revolution, which occurred on July 14, 1789. This meant that Chung had only a few months to get things together. The new building was not yet complete. The opera, which would open the celebration, had been changed. And the fast approaching opera season had to be organized.

Chung's assignment was to create an opera company that would give up to 250 performances in one year and whose opening would mark a new beginning for France's place in the arts. Into this arena, Chung strode confidently. A man of three continents — Korean by birth, American by citizenship, and European by current employment — he felt he was just the person for this challenge.

When the curtain finally rose on March 17, 1990, everything seemed ready. And when the curtain came down everyone agreed that the performance of *Les Troyens* was nothing short of triumphant. The man whose mission had been compared to "taking command of the *Titanic* after it hit the iceberg" turned out to be a brilliant captain. All seemed confident the ship would sail!

Yo-Yo Ma
Cellist
1955

"**W**hen I give a concert, I like to think that I'm welcoming someone to my home," Yo-Yo Ma said recently before going on stage at one of Europe's great concert halls. "I've lived with the music a long time; it's an old friend, and I want to say, 'Let's all participate.'"

Born in Paris, France, in 1955, Yo-Yo was the second child of Hiao-Tsiun (a professor of music) and Marina Ma (a singer). His parents moved to Europe in the 1930s when China's government was going through radical change. As very young children, Yo-Yo and his sister, Yeou-Cheng were tutored by their father in history, Chinese literature, and calligraphy (elegant handwriting). Each child also played an instrument. Yeou-Cheng played the violin and Yo-Yo, the cello.

Hiao-Tsiun's method for teaching young children was simple. He gave them very short lessons, which were to be learned thoroughly. Every day four-year-old Yo-Yo was expected to memorize two measures of Bach. Day by day, two measures at a time, he learned to understand the pattern of Bach and slowly began to understand musical structure. As he grew older and was expected to learn complicated pieces quickly, he applied the basic principle learned from his father: break up the problem into four parts and approach each without fear. After the parts are learned, put them all back together, and you will have mastered what you thought was too complex.

Using this process, Yo-Yo progressed in music so rapidly that, at the age of five, he gave his first public concert at the University of Paris.

In 1962 the Ma family went to New York City to help in a family emergency. Although they intended to return to Paris in a few months, their stay in America became permanent. In New York, Yo-Yo's musical talent flourished. Soon he was studying with the most distinguished cellists and began performing with orchestras around the world. This freedom and a stressful homelife, however, began to take its toll on him. Yo-Yo's father, who believed strongly in Chinese values, began strictly enforcing them on his free-spirited, Americanized son. The restrictions caused serious conflicts that Yo-Yo had difficulty dealing with.

"My home life was totally structured," he recalls. As a result, "because I couldn't rebel there, I did so at school." Soon the once perfect student began missing classes and snapping back at his teachers. Once considered a genius, Yo-Yo was now gaining a reputation as a goof-off. He seemed confused about who he was and what he should do with his life.

In an effort to deal with the problem, Yo-Yo moved to Boston, Massachusetts, where he enrolled at Harvard University. There he combined a rigorous liberal arts program with a career as a concert cellist. Between classes and exams, he jetted off to world capitals to perform as a soloist with great orchestras. With his father's guidance, he learned how to balance his time between music engagements and his college education.

Shortly after graduating from Harvard in 1977, Yo-Yo married Jill Horner, and they settled in the Boston area. Today the Mas have two children and try hard to lead a normal life — when Yo-Yo is at home, that is. He is much in demand as both a soloist and a recording artist.

David Henry Hwang
Playwright
1957

"You can't trust appearances," is the message of David Henry Hwang's plays. People may look Asian, African, European, masculine, or feminine and may act a certain way, but the observer may be wrong. The outcome of Hwang's award-winning play *M Butterfly*, about a French diplomat's love for a Chinese actress, startled many audiences with this profound message.

Born in Los Angeles, California, in 1957, David Hwang grew up in a wealthy suburb. His father, a native of Shanghai, China, was the president of a bank in Los Angeles's Chinatown. Both his parents had come to the United States from China in the 1940s, yet David's upbringing was so all-American that he rarely thought about being Asian. He knew he was Chinese, he once said, but it seemed a minor detail, like, perhaps, the color of his hair.

David's strongest awareness of his Chinese heritage came from his grandmother who always told wonderful stories about the family's ancestors in China. When he was twelve years old, he started to write these stories down. Later, like fellow Chinese writer, Maxine Hong Kingston, he incorporated many of the traditional stories he learned about China into his own writing.

After graduating from a Los Angeles area prep school, David attended Stanford University, where he majored in English and became interested in theatre. At Stanford, he also tried his hand at playwriting, which, he says, "seemed to me the most magical form. . . . I knew I wanted to write things to create worlds and then see the worlds right in front of me."

Hwang's first play, written while he was still a student, was called *F.O.B.* — the acronym for "fresh off the boat" — an unflattering name for a new arrival to America. The play, which is about the clash between a "fresh-off-the-boat" Chinese man and his American cousin, was well received in San Francisco. Eventually, it also opened in New York City, where it won an Obie Award for the best off-Broadway play of the 1980-81 season.

While a student at Yale School of Drama, Hwang wrote *The Dance and the Railroad,* a play about the Chinese immigrants who built the first transcontinental railroad in the United States. He wrote the play to change the historical image of Chinese workers as unskilled "little coolies." *The Dance and the Railroad* focuses on two men, who, during a long labor strike, practice the complicated dance movements of the Chinese opera. The two men seem to have little in common but do share a dream of returning to China to perform with the Beijing Opera.

Several years after a successful New York run of *The Dance and the Railroad*, David Henry Hwang's play *M Butterfly* opened. Based on the true-life story of a French diplomat who is in love with a Chinese actress, the play explores the way strong emotions and prejudices hide the truth from people. The Frenchman, who claims he knew nothing about the actress's sexual identity or true profession, is eventually found guilty of passing state secrets to his mistress, who turns out to be not only a Chinese intelligence agent but also a man.

Since *M Butterfly* opened in 1988, it has won several major awards, including a Tony Award for the best Broadway play of the year, and has played to packed theatres around the world.

Today David Henry Hwang lives in New York City where he writes for theatre, film, and television.

Vietnamese refugees sit in Cambodian waters after being denied entry into Thailand in 1977

Vietnamese Boat People

The Vietnam War ended when Communist forces conquered South Vietnam, Laos, and Cambodia in 1975. A new drama then began as the people of the defeated nations struggled to free themselves from harsh Communist rule. Some people fled to the jungles and joined armed resistance groups. Others chose to abandon their homelands altogether and emigrate elsewhere.

Beginning in the mid-1970s, hundreds of thousands of people fled South Vietnam. These desperate refugees came from all walks of life, including government officials, doctors, merchants, and ordinary laborers. Most people tried to escape with their entire families. Unfortunately, many did not make it out alive.

The escape route chosen by most was extremely perilous: by boat over the South China Sea. Vietnamese shores were carefully guarded against such escapes, so those who actually succeeded did so with careful planning and a lot of luck. One man, a teacher named Phuong Hoang, bought a small fishing boat with a friend. For an entire year they secretly posed as fishermen so they could learn how to navigate on the open sea. Phuong did not even reveal his escape plan to his family. Schoolteachers were known to be notorious government informers, and he feared that his children might innocently let news of the plan slip out in school. Being discovered could have serious consequences.

In 1976 Phuong finally managed to escape. He and his friend told their families to dress in swimsuits for a day of fun on the boat. Since they carried no luggage or extra supplies, the police were not suspicious. Once everyone was aboard, Hoang turned on the engine and sped from the shore as fast as he could. The eight people spent four fearful days on the open water. Dozens of ships passed, ignoring their S.O.S. signals. Finally, after a journey of more than 900 miles (1,450 km), they were rescued by an Italian oil tanker and then transported to Saudi Arabia where they escaped to Canada and to freedom.

Phuong Hoang's story is one of incredible luck. Many thousands were not so fortunate. They rode rickety boats that sunk at sea, or were set upon by pirates who robbed and raped them. Many died of hunger, dehydration, or exposure to the sun. Some escapees were detained by border guards before leaving Vietnam. Those who were lucky enough to escape and arrive at safe harbors in Indonesia, the Philippines, Taiwan, and Hong Kong were denied entry into the country because of immigration quotas. Many refugees intentionally sunk their boats upon arrival so the authorities could not send them back. By 1979 government policies began to change and more refugees were allowed to emigrate to the West.

Vietnamese refugees arrive in Pulau Bidong, Malaysia, in 1979

Most of the people who fled Vietnam hoped to make the United States their final destination. Because of U. S. quota restrictions, however, many were not accepted. As late as 1977, only three hundred Asian immigrants were allowed into the United States every month. After 1977 quotas were increased with restrictions, however. Immigrants had to be close relatives of U. S. citizens, former top officials of the defeated South Vietnamese government, or people who had collaborated with the United States during the war.

Once in the United States, even rich, important, and highly educated immigrants had to start careers in low-level, low-paying jobs. For a decade, former South Vietnamese Prime Minister Hguyen Cao Ky lived quietly in

Former South Vietnamese Prime Minister Nguyen Cao Ky at his shrimp processing plant in Dulac, Louisiana, in 1988

Louisiana trying to run a liquor store and then a fishing business. After declaring bankruptcy, he moved near Los Angeles, California, where he lives with a sister in a Vietnamese community. Since relocating to California, he has been publicly advocating diplomatic and economic pressure on the Hanoi government to bring about democracy and freedom in Vietnam.

Adapting to the climate and customs of America has been difficult for Vietnamese immigrants. They have had to learn a new language while earning a living in a complex economy and adjusting to values that are very different from their own. Many feel that the very fabric of the Vietnamese family is being torn apart. Parents are desperately clinging to traditional values while their children are rebelling.

For example, in Vietnam most marriages are arranged by the parents when their children are very young; but in America the adult children are choosing their own husbands and wives. In Vietnam families live in close proximity to each other; but in America many adult children are choosing to live far from their families and visiting their parents infrequently, if at all.

Like many other immigrant communities who are struggling to survive in America, the Vietnamese are having to deal with corruption, crime, and violence working their way into the fabric of their culture. In August 1979, a dispute between immigrant Vietnamese fishermen and residents of Seadrift, Texas, exploded when an American fisherman was killed and several Vietnamese fishing boats were firebombed in retaliation. In the 1980s, Vietnamese street gangs were caught extorting money from local businesses and harassing ordinary citizens.

As first and second generation Vietnamese Americans join mainstream America, however, there are strong signs that life is improving for them. In urban communites such as Little Saigon, a bustling section of Orange County, California, young and old Vietnamese Americans are succeeding in American jobs and still maintaining their traditional customs. In schools, there is evidence of more children participating in traditional Vietnamese festivals. In shopping malls more stores owned by Vietnamese are opening for business.

Although more than a half-million refugees have emigrated to the United States since the end of the Vietnam War, many more are still waiting to come. The strict Communist regime in Vietnam continues to make life difficult. As the immigration waiting lists continue to grow, more people still attempt the dangerous escape from their homeland.

A busy market in the Michoud Area of New Orleans where many Vietnamese have settled

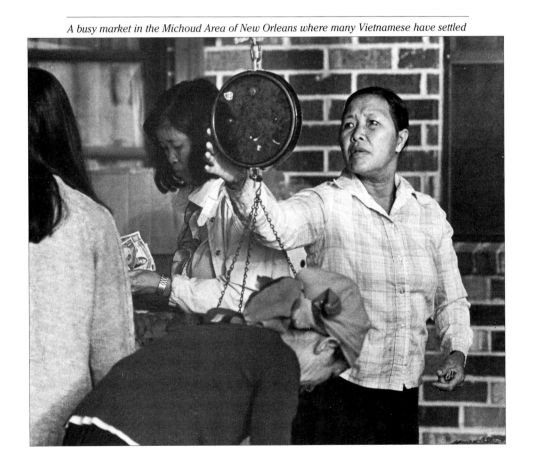

*A Hmong mother and her children huddle near a fireplace
at a refugee summer camp in Issaquah, Washington.*

The Hmong: Refugees from Laos

At an early age, Hmong girls are taught the art of *pa ndau,* a dazzling, intricate type of embroidery. In traditional Hmong culture, a girl's skill at *pa ndau* determines the wealth of her future husband. Since 1975, when the Hmong were forced to flee their mountainous homeland in Laos, Hmong women have used their embroidery to tell stories of their refugee experience. Their delicate stitchery shows the Hmong running from Vietnamese soldiers, crossing the Mekong River, and walking hundreds of miles to a refugee camp in Thailand. The final scene depicts the long voyage to the United States.

The Hmong are one of three tribes called the *Lao Soung,* "people of the mountain." Migrating to Laos from China about 150 years ago, most settled in the northeastern plateau of Xieng Khouang Province. (Laos is a Southeast Asian country sandwiched between Vietnam and Thailand. To the south lies Cambodia. China is to the north.)

During the war between the United States and Vietnam in the 1960s and 1970s, the United States employed many Hmong men as guerrilla fighters. When the war ended with the defeat of the U. S.-backed forces, the Hmong were forced to flee Laos, which had been taken over by the Vietnamese communists. During the evacuation, many Hmong were killed by Vietnamese soldiers, others escaped by walking hundreds of miles through jungles to a refugee camp in Thailand. From there, many began the long voyage across the Pacific Ocean.

Today there are more than one hundred thousand Hmong living in the United States, primarily in California, Minnesota, Wisconsin, and North Carolina. Adjustments to resettlement have been difficult. One of the greatest problems has been language — not only English but also *Meo-Yao,* their own language. Until very recently, Meo-Yao was only a spoken language and, therefore, did not have its own alphabet. As a result, most refugees cannot read or write. And being illiterate in their own language makes learning a new one doubly hard.

In Laos Hmong survival did not depend on their ability to read or write but on how successful they were at farming and raising livestock to feed their families. Because they lived on remote mountainsides and had little contact with outsiders, the Hmong had no need for currency or the kind of rules and regulations Westerners rely on. Because plumbing and technological advances had not reached them, they were unaware of their uses and applications.

In America, however, understandings and expectations are very different. Education is the key to economic prosperity. Highly formalized and competitive procedures for buying and selling are the rule. And high tech products and systems are practically considered necessities. It's not surprising then that Hmong refugees would find life in America difficult to understand and adapt to.

The ability to work is one of the highest priorities in Hmong society. Because many refugees cannot find work in America, they sit in government-owned apartments, confused by their new surroundings, and with little hope for the future. Such a drastic change in lifestyle actually seems to be killing many healthy Hmong men. Sudden Unexplained Death Syndrome (SUDS) is the name of the ailment that has taken the lives of many. Medical experts believe that extreme culture shock might be the cause of it.

Nearly twenty years after the Vietnam War and the arrival of the first group of Hmong to the United States, they are adapting slowly. Parents watch with a mixture of delight and fear as their children learn English and become productive Americans. They're happy the future will be brighter for them but are concerned that they are losing respect for their traditional culture and customs.

Some might wonder if older Hmong will ever truly become Americans or if they are just waiting for the Communist government in Laos to collapse so they can return to their mountain homes. Yang Dao, who lives in Minnesota and recently received a Ph. D., is optimistic. "It is only here, in the United States that the Hmong are able to learn that the young can go to school and become important members of a society," he says. "Even if we some day go back to Laos, we will have the tools to play an important part in the action and not have to stick to the mountains. . . ."

A Hmong artist proudly displays a traditional embroidery

Maya Ying Lin
Architect, Sculptor
1960

When Maya Lin was twenty-one years old and a senior at Yale University in Connecticut, she entered a national contest to design a monument in Washington, D.C. that would honor the veterans of the Vietnam War and provide a place where people could come to deal with the anger and pain the war created.

Ms. Lin's design was a simple pastel drawing of a black V-shaped wall tucked into the side of a small hill. Carved on the wall's black granite surface were the names of more than 58,000 men and women who died during the war. Her design, which was among 1,420 other contest entries, was unanimously chosen for its simplicity and strength.

The Vietnam Veterans Memorial opened on Veteran's Day, 1982. Since then more than a million people have stood before the names. They come to cry, and think, and touch the cold black granite. The presence of so many people makes the wall truly a living memorial to the war's dead.

Maya Ying Lin was born in Athens, Ohio, in 1960. Her parents had fled Shanghai, China, in the late 1940s. After arriving in the United States, they both accepted teaching positions at Ohio University. Maya's father was the university's dean of fine arts until his death in 1989. Her mother still teaches English and Oriental literature at the university.

Maya attended Yale University as both an undergraduate and, later, a graduate student in architecture. Unlike most students, who worry about

A veteran and his son at the Vietnam Veterans Memorial in Washington, D.C.

finding the right job after graduation, Maya was well established in her field when she left school. Her winning design of the Vietnam Veterans Memorial brought her national recognition.

After having completed work on the Vietnam Memorial, Lin settled into a career as an architect and sculptor. She had decided not to design any more memorials, but changed her mind after receiving a call in 1988 from the Southern Poverty Law Center in Montgomery, Alabama. The center's directors wanted to build a civil rights memorial that would occupy the plaza in front of their headquarters in Montgomery.

Maya spent months studying about the civil rights movement and, as she said, "waiting for a form to show up." Finally, she came across a biblical phrase that was used in two speeches given by Martin Luther King, Jr.: "We will not be satisfied until justice rolls down like waters and righteousness like a mighty stream." After reading those words, Lin knew that water would be a part of the monument. She decided to make a time line of the movement's major events, including the killings of forty men, women, and children, and cover the words with a fine layer of water. Like the Vietnam Veterans Memorial, visitors are invited to touch the carved granite and, in a sense, join hands with the dead. The Civil Rights Memorial was dedicated in the fall of 1989.

Today Maya Lin works as both an architect and a sculptor. She lives in New York City.

Eugene H. Trinh

Physicist, Astronaut
1950

O n July 4, 1992, Eugene Trinh helped the United States celebrate its 216th birthday. He and other members of the Space Shuttle *Columbia* crew traveling in space set off sparklers and then sang a rousing version of "The Star Spangled Banner." For Dr. Trinh, the first Vietnamese American to fly on a U. S. spacecraft, it was, to say the least, a memorable occasion.

When Eugene was born in 1950, Vietnam was called French Indochina and was engaged in a bloody war with France. (This war, which had begun in 1946, would end with the French leaving the country in 1954.) To escape the violence and social upheaval, the Trinh family moved to Paris in 1952.

Eugene attended French elementary schools, where, right from the start, he distinguished himself in math and science. In 1968 he graduated from Paris's Lycee Michelet, one of the city's most respected high schools. New York City's Columbia University lured him away from Europe with an offer of a full scholarship.

Four years later, he graduated from Columbia with a degree in mechanical engineering and applied physics. At Yale University, Trinh completed his doctoral degree in applied physics and then began working with the U. S. space agency, NASA.

Dr. Trinh's research is in acoustics, which is the science of sound. (An accoustical specialist tests the effects of sound and sound waves on various materials in different environments.) For both NASA and the Jet Propulsion Laboratory in Pasadena, California, Dr. Trinh developed experiments that could be performed on space flights.

These experiments have involved testing high-temperature materials in both low-gravity and normal conditions. Of particular interest to Dr. Trinh's research are the effects of low gravity over time. The *Columbia* Space Shuttle's mission, which was to stay in orbit longer than any previous shuttle flight, would provide Dr. Trinh the perfect opportunity to test his research.

While in orbit, Dr. Trinh performed experiments that tested what happens to fire in a weightless environment. One of his broad goals was to observe whether the low-gravity experience in outer space can offer scientists clues to the causes of earth's serious environmental problems. The mission, which ended on July 10, 1992, was proclaimed a great success.

Eugene Trinh and his wife, Yvette, a native of France, live in Culver City, California. When Dr. Trinh isn't working at his lab in Pasadena, he likes to tinker around his house or play tennis in the warm California sun.

Greg Louganis
Olympic Diver
1960

After competing in three Olympics and more than ten world championships, Greg Louganis knew that the next dive would prove whether or not he was a true champion. He had already completed nine out of ten dives and was still in second place in the platform competition of the 1988 Summer Olympics. As he walked up the ladder to the platform, he tried not to look at Xiong Ni, the fourteen-year-old Chinese boy who was in first place, or to think that this was his last Olympic dive and that it had to be nothing short of perfect. Instead, he pictured the dive in his mind. He saw himself at the edge of the concrete, his arms rising like the wings of a bird. . . .

Minutes later, as Greg climbed out of the pool, the computer flashed his score. The audience roared as they realized this great champion had won another gold medal, becoming the first man in history to win two gold medals in back-to-back Olympics. Then the man, who one journalist described as "running on pure courage," broke down and cried.

"Pure courage" was something Greg had drawn on many times during his troubled youth. His parents were very young when Greg was born and decided to give him up for adoption. Peter and Frances Louganis, his adoptive parents, provided a loving home for Greg and his sister, Despina, who had been adopted earlier. But early on, learning difficulties and feelings of not belonging began surfacing in Greg.

School was a constant source of frustration for him. Being of Samoan ancestry, he was teased about his dark features. He felt as if he were an outsider. And to make matters worse, he had trouble reading. He struggled to make sense out of words that appeared to be just a jumble of letters. In time, teachers realized that Greg had a reading disorder called dyslexia, which caused him to reverse letters and words.

As an athelete, however, Greg was able to outperform anyone. He excelled at gymnastics and began diving at age nine. By eleven, he was chosen for the Junior Olympics in Colorado. And by the time he was in junior high school, he was considered one of America's best young divers.

On a springboard, he could jump higher than others and, with the extra height, could stay in the air longer. His dives never looked rushed. Greg also had superb concentration, which allowed him to clear his head and focus on one dive at a time.

Back at school, however, no one cared much about his diving skills. While trying desperately to make friends, he got in with the "wrong crowd." Then he began to lose interest in diving. Concerned about Greg's well-being, his parents contacted Dr. Sammy Lee, a former Olympic champion who often coached promising young divers. Dr. Lee saw that Greg's talent was truly extraordinary and offered to become both his coach and guardian. After the Louganis family accepted Lee's offer, Greg's life changed.

Dr. Lee was able to communiciate with Greg as few others could. He, too, had been called names because of his Asian ancestry. Dr. Lee's parents, however, who had both been born in Korea, had taught him that when others look down at you, you must work doubly hard.

With Dr. Lee's guidance, Greg prepared himself for world competition. At sixteen he won a silver medal at the 1976 Olympics in Montreal. By 1978 he had won the first of many world titles. Then in 1984 he won two Olympic gold medals in Los Angeles. According to press reports he had truly become one of America's heroes.

No one anticipated that he could win again — not even Greg himself. But as the 1988 Summer Olympic Games in Seoul, Korea, approached, he felt the pull of competition drawing him back. And once again he came out on top.

After his stunning double victory in Seoul, Greg Louganis was elevated to a position among the true heroes of sport. As he neared thirty, he retired from diving competition and today lives in Malibu, California.

Andy Leonard
Power Weightlifter
1968

"**C**'mon Andy!" shouted friends from the audience, as Andy Leonard walked out onto the raised platform at the International Special Olympics Summer Games. He stepped up to the bar, stretched his arms over his head, and prepared to pick up — "deadlift" — 402 pounds (182 kg).

Andy pulled at the bar and, for a few seconds, it looked as though he couldn't possibly budge it. Then he began to lift the bar from the platform. He brought it to the middle of his thigh and the referee signaled that the lift was complete. As Andy let go of the bar, it crashed to the floor. When the crowd jumped to its feet and applauded wildly, he smiled and flashed the number one sign.

Andy Leonard's success story began at Happy Place, the English name for the An Lac Orphanage in Saigon, South Vietnam, where he grew up. And indeed, An Lac did bring a measure of happiness to his sad, shattered childhood. It helped him survive and gave him an opportunity for a future in America.

Born in 1968, during the height of America's involvement in the Vietnam War, Andy lost both of his parents during a rocket blast on his native village. Afterward, he and his four brothers and sisters were taken to the An Lac Orphanage. Not long after they arrived, Andy's siblings ran away, leaving him — still a toddler — behind.

Even though the orphanage was a haven during the war, children still witnessed frequent air raids and enemy fire. In the spring of 1975, as the Americans were withdrawing from Vietnam and the Communist forces were moving into the capital, U. S. officials agreed to evacuate the city's orphanages. Operation Babylift, as it was called, took place on April 12. Two cargo planes left Saigon for the Philippines; among their passengers were 219 crying An Lac children, one of whom was Andy Leonard.

Shortly after their arrival in Fort Bening, Georgia, Richard Leonard, a Methodist minister from Lock Haven, Pennsylvania, received a late-night phone call. Was he still interested in adopting a Vietnamese orphan? Richard answered a resounding "Yes," and he and his wife, Irene, immediately left for Georgia.

When the Leonards first saw Andy, he looked "like a piece of tagged luggage." Lost and forlorn, he had a scrap of paper pinned to his chest on which someone had scribbled "Leonard."

Andy's adjustment to American life was difficult. He suffered from nightmares and often woke up crying. At first he wouldn't eat, and then he began hoarding food out of fear that he might never have enough. Andy struggled in school, too. Finally, doctors reached the conclusion that untreated ear infections as an infant had damaged Andy's brain and left him learning disabled.

But outside the classroom, Andy competed successfully in a variety of sports, including soccer, swimming, and baseball. His height soon became a problem, however. Only five feet tall by the age of sixteen, Andy was often cut from teams that wanted taller, stronger players. So the Leonards steered him in the direction of Special Olympics competition when he began excelling.

When Andy's Special Olympics athletics coach introduced him to a powerlifter, Andy was immediately intrigued with the idea of lifting as much weight as possible. His coach, Clyde Doll, decided Andy was sturdy enough to give it a try so he loaded a bar with 40 pounds (18 kg) and told him to do some presses. The coach expected Andy to do six or eight. Andy completed twenty.

Encouraged by Andy's ability, Coach Doll entered him in some regular local meets. Andy finished second in his first meet. Since then, he has competed in various meets sponsored by the American Drug-Free Powerlifting Association (ADFPA), which opposes the use of steroids. He has won the Pennsylvania championships twice. In the Special Olympics he holds records for bench press, squat, and deadlift.

Today Andy lives on his own in State College, Pennsylvania, not far from his parents. He works at a restaurant and trains daily in a gym. He helps Coach Doll train other Special Olympic athletes who consider him their role model. Andy Leonard's life is about more than brute strength. It is an extraordinary example of courage and personal achievement.

Midori
Violinist
1971

Midori wasn't quite ten when, in 1981, she was invited to perform at the Aspen Music Festival before an audience of fellow musicians. As she took center stage, many wondered how such a tiny girl could even hold a violin, much less play one. The great violinist, Pinchas Zukerman, recalled:

> "I was sitting on a chair, and I was as tall as she was standing. She tuned, she bowed to the audience, she bowed to me, she bowed to the pianist — and then she played the Bartok concerto. . . . I sat there and tears started coming down my cheeks. . . . I was absolutely stunned. I turned to the audience and said, 'Ladies and gentlemen, I don't know about you, but I've just witnessed a miracle."[14]

Born in Osaka, Japan, in 1971, Midori Goto began violin lessons shortly after her third birthday. Even before that, however, music was part of her life. She often waited in auditoriums while her mother, a concert violinist and teacher named Setsu Goto, gave classes and rehearsed. Midori's mother knew early on that her young daughter was deeply sensitive to music.

In 1982, just shy of Midori's eleventh birthday, Setsu decided to leave Japan and enroll her daughter at The Juilliard School in New York City. While studying music at Juilliard, Midori also attended The Professional Children's School, a unique college preparatory school for children in the arts. It was here at The Children's School that she learned English and received her academic education.

The adjustment to American culture for the Goto family was difficult, yet they were willing to make the necessary sacrifices for Midori's promising career. Her leap to the ranks of the world's great violinists seemed only a few years away.

By the time Midori was sixteen and still a student at Juilliard, she began appearing with orchestras in packed concert halls around the world. Audiences were thrilled with this tiny girl and her huge talent. Yet her mother and manager agreed Midori's career should not take off too fast. Believing that Midori needed more time to learn and mature, they decided to put off her solo debut.

In 1987 Midori made the controversial decision to leave The Juilliard School and prepare for her professional recital debut. Although she remained at The Professional Children's School, where she graduated in 1990, leaving The Juilliard School allowed Midori the time she needed to prepare for her debut and accept invitations to perform with the world's great orchestras.

When the time came for Midori's debut, she chose New York's Carnegie Hall where so many great violinists, such as Jascha Heifitz and Yehudi Menuhin, had made their starts while still quite young. Midori knew that to be forever compared with the greats, her recital would need to be perfect.

The recital date was set for October 25, 1990 — just a few days after her nineteenth birthday. Despite the pressure, Midori was poised and confident. After all, Midori had been preparing for this moment since the time she first played her tiny violin for her mother. There was no way she was going to ruin the most important night of her life.

Carnegie Hall was sold out. Representatives from the Sony Corporation were there to make both a videotape and compact disc, yet Midori was cool and calm. Part of the reason, Midori explained, is that on stage she is truly at home. "I feel so comfortable onstage; I feel safest. The best part of giving concerts is just being out there and playing, nothing else." When the evening was over, critics pronounced the recital a "triumph."

Today Midori is in such demand as a soloist that she can be touring full time. However, she prefers to stay close to her adopted hometown, New York City, where she lives with her mother, stepfather, and younger brother.

Midori playing with the Boston Symphony Orchestra at the Tanglewood Music Festival July 26, 1986

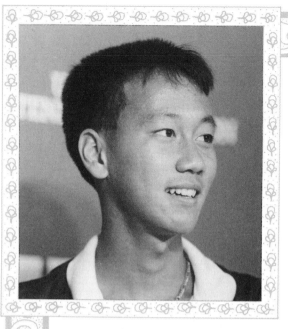

Michael Chang
Tennis Player
1972

"**T**hese two weeks are going to stay with me the rest of my life," said Michael Chang after winning the French Open tennis tournament in June 1989. He was only seventeen and had just become both the youngest male ever to win a Grand Slam tournament and the first American to win the French Open in more than forty years.

Michael was used to being the "youngest ever." At fifteen, he was the youngest to win a pro tournament, then the youngest male to win a singles match at the U. S. Open. The following year, he was the youngest to play on center court at Wimbledon. So winning a Grand Slam tournament at seventeen seemed right on schedule.

Soon after Michael was born on February 22, 1972, Michael's father, Joe, began preparing his two sons for tennis. Mr. Chang was so enthusiastic about the game of tennis, which he began to play in 1974, that he decided everyone in the family should learn it. Michael was six years old when he first started to play tennis. A year later, he had won his first tournament.

Tennis remained a family affair as Michael progressed through the ranks of top junior players. The Changs moved from Minnesota to Placentia, California, so Michael could play year round. Although Joe Chang worked full time as a chemist, he continued to be Michael's primary coach. An extremely organized man, Mr. Chang used training data plus his own readings and observations to plot out Michael's entire career. He decided in which tournaments his son should play and, later, when Michael should turn pro.

In 1988 Michael, an honor student at Placentia High School scored well on a high school proficiency test and graduated two years early — in time for his professional debut. That same year, his mother Betty quit her job as a research chemist to travel on the professional tour with him. She did his laundry, cooked his favorite Chinese meals, gave him encouragement and, perhaps most importantly, saw to it that after his day of tennis, he could pursue his second favorite sport — fishing.

Michael Chang is in many ways an unlikely sports champion. Quiet, reflective, "a nice kid," as many call him, he likes to spend his spare time browsing in book stores or enjoying the peace and quiet of nature. "Just being out there is comforting." he once said about fishing.

More often, however, Michael Chang is "out there" in front of 30,000 fans on a tennis court. Since winning the French Open in 1989, neither the public nor the press has wanted to leave Michael Chang alone. His love for tennis seems unchanged, but the attention has created rough patches in his career. He had hoped to settle comfortably into tennis's top ten players. Instead, he has moved up and down in the rankings, losing several tournaments he was favored to win. The pressures of being a young celebrity have been a factor in Michael Chang's uneven play, despite his family's efforts to protect him. One sports magazine called Michael Chang America's tennis hope for the 1990s, and Michael intends to prove that forecast right.

Kristi Yamaguchi

Figure Skater

1971

The 1992 Albertville Winter Olympics in France were Kristi Yamaguchi's first Olympic competition for the United States. Not many expected her to win a medal. The experience was just supposed to prepare Kristi for the 1994 Olympics in Lillihamer, Norway, where many hoped she would take the gold. But to the delight of Americans and her doting fans, Kristi Yamaguchi returned to California with a 1992 gold medal that proved everyone wrong.

Kristi was born in Fremont, California, in 1971. Her parents, Carole and Jim Yamaguchi, are third-generation Japanese Americans. Although the Yamaguchis have been in the United States for four generations, they carry scars from anti-Japanese discrimination. Mrs. Yamaguchi was born in a Colorado internment camp, where her family had been sent after the Japanese attack on Pearl Harbor in 1941. Like many Japanese Americans at the time, her parents lost their home and their business (a flower farm) when they were imprisoned. Mr. Yamaguchi's family's story is similar. Yet neither of the Yamaguchis dwell on their hardships. Instead, they prefer to talk about their children, who they describe as Californians in love with the outdoors and excelling in such things as skateboarding, baton twirling, basketball, and figure skating.

Kristi began skating at the age of six and was "a natural" on ice. By the time she was eight, she was training with Canadian coach Christy Kjarsgaard.

And a few years later, she began skating with a partner, Rudi Galindo. In 1986 they won the U. S. Pairs Championship. The same year, Kristi also placed fourth in the singles competition.

In 1989 Kristi became the first woman to compete in both the singles and pairs events at the World Championships. Having already placed first in pairs and second in singles earlier that year at the U. S. Championships, she placed fifth in pairs and sixth in singles at the World Championships.

A day after graduating from high school, Kristi moved to Edmonton, Canada, where her coach had moved. She resumed her singles training, deciding to devote herself entirely to figure skating. She achieved that goal sooner than anyone expected when she won a gold medal at the 1991 World Championships in Munich, Germany. That win gave her the recognition she deserved and catapulted her into the 1992 Winter Olympics.

On the final day of Olympic competition, Ms. Yamaguchi skated two clean programs to take the gold. A month later, in Oakland, California, Ms. Yamaguchi again won the World Championships. She was truly figure skating's reigning queen and America's newest sweetheart.

Kristi Yamaguchi competing at the 1992 Winter Olympics

Notes

[1] Betty Lee Sung, *Mountain of Gold: The Story of Chinese in America* (New York: Macmillan, 1967), p. 24.

[2] Ibid.

[3] L.C. Tsung, *The Marginal Man* (reprinted in *The Chinese Americans* by Milton Meltzer, New York: Thomas Y. Crowell), pp. 91–92.

[4] *Mountain of Gold*, p. 195.

[5] Edward Joesting. *Kauai: The Separate Kingdom*. (Hawaii: University of Hawaii Press), p. 34.

[6] Carlos Bulosan, *America Is in the Heart* (Seattle: University of Washington Press, 1973), p. 236.

[7] Craig Sharlin and Lilia V. Villanueva, *Philip Vera Cruz: A Personal History of Filipino Immigrants and the Farmworkers Movement* (Los Angeles: UCLA Labor Center, Institute of Industrial Relations and UCLA Asian American Studies Center, 1992), p. 146.

[8] Deborah Gesensway and Mindy Roseman, *Beyond Words: Images from America's Concentration Camps* (Itasca, New York: Cornell University Press, 1987), p. 18–19.

[9] Ibid., p. 56

[10] Commission on Wartime Relocations and Internment of Civilians, *Personal Justice Denied* (Washington, D.C.: Government Printing Office, 1982), p. 18.

[11] Luoth Yin (by permission of author)

[12] Louth Yin (by permission of author)

[13] Janet Nomura Morey and Wendy Dunn, *Famous Asian Americans* (New York: Dutton/Cobblehill Books, 1992), pp. 126–127.

[14] K. Robert Schwarz, *"Glissando"* (*New York Times Magazine*, March 24, 1991), p. 32.

Further Reading

Biography

Bode, Janet. *New Kids on the Block: Oral Histories of Immigrant Teens*. New York: Franklin Watts, 1989.

Endo, Takako, et al. *Japanese American Journey: The Story of a People*. San Mateo, CA: JACP, 1985.

Fiffer, Sharon Sloan. *Imagining America: Paul Thai's Journey from the Killing Fields of Cambodia to Freedom in the U.S.A.*, New York: Paragon, 1992.

Fritz, Jean. *Homesick: My Own Story*. New York: Putnam, 1982.

Gesensway, Deborah and Mindy Roseman. *Beyond Words: Images from America's Concentration Camps*. Itasca, New York: Cornell University Press, 1987.

Hamanaka, Sheila. *The Journey: Japanese Americans, Racism, and Renewal*. New York: Orchard Press, 1990.

Houston, Jeanne Wakutsuki and James D. Houston. *Farewell to Manzanar*. New York: Bantam, 1973.

Huynh, Quang Nhuong. *The Land I Lost: Adventures of a Boy in Vietnam*. New York: Harper and Row, 1982.

Ignacio, Melissa Macagba. *The Philippines: Roots of My Heritage*. San Jose, California: Filipino Development Associates, Inc., 1977.

Ishikawa, Yoshimi. *Strawberry Road: A Japanese Immigrant Discovers America*. Tr. by Eve Zimmerman. Kodansha, 1991.

Moore, David L. *Dark Sky, Dark Land: Stories of the Hmong Boy Scouts of Troop 100*. Minnesota: Eden Prentice, 1989.

Morey, Janet Nomura and Wendy Dunn. *Famous Asian Americans*. New York: Dutton/Cobblehill, 1992.

Noguchi, Isamu. *Isamu Noguchi: A Sculptor's World*. New York: Harper and Row, 1968.

Ogawa, Dennis M. and Glen Grant. *Ellison Onizuka: A Remembrance.* Hawaii: The Onizuka Memorial Committee, 1986.

Stanley, Fay. *The Last Princess: The Story of Princess Kiulani of Hawaii.* New York: MacMillan, 1991

Uchida, Yoshiko. *The Invisible Thread.* New York: Charles Messner, 1991.

Waters, Kate and Madeline Slovenz-Low. *Lion Dancer: Ernie Wan's Chinese New Year.* New York: Scholastic, 1990.

Yung, Judy. *Chinese Women of America: A Pictorial History.* Seattle, Washington: University of Washington Press, 1986.

History

Ashabranner, Brent. *The New Americans: Changing Patterns in U. S. Immigration* . New York: Dodd, Mead, 1983.

Ashabranner, Brent and Melissa Ashabranner. *Into a Strange Land: Unaccompanied Refugee Youth in America.* New York: Dodd, Mead, 1987.

Asch, Carol. *The Social and Psychological Adjustment of Southeast Asian Refugees.* New York: Teachers College, Columbia University, 1982.

Bong-youn Choy. *Koreans in America.* Chicago: Nelson-Hall, 1979.

Brownstone, David. *The Chinese-American Heritage.* New York: Facts on File Publications, 1988.

Davis, Daniel S. *Behind Barbed Wire: The Imprisonment of Japanese Americans During World War II.* New York: E. P. Dutton, 1982.

Kitano, Harry. *The Japanese Americans.* New York: Chelsea House, 1987.

Kitano, Harry and Roger Daniels. *Asian Americans: Emerging Minorities.* New Jersey: Prentice Hall, 1988.

Knoll, Tricia. *Becoming American: Asian Sojourners, Immigrants, and Refugees in the Western U. S.* Portland, Oregon: Coast to Coast Books, 1982.

Lasker, Bruno. *Filipino Immigration to the Continental United States and Hawaii.* Chicago: University of Chicago Press, 1931.

Meltzer, Milton. *The Chinese Americans.* Thomas Y. Crowell, 1980.

Liu, William. *Tradition to Nowhere: Vietnam Refugees in America.* New York: Charter Spring, 1979.

McCunn, Ruthanne Lum. *Chinese American Portraits: Personal Histories 1828-1988.* Chronicle Press, 1988.

McCunn, Ruthanne Lum. *Thousand Pieces of Gold.* Design Enterprises of San Francisco, 1981.

Mc Williams, Carey. *Brothers Under the Skin.* Boston: Little, brown, 1943.

Sing, Bill, ed. *Asian-Pacific Americans.* Los Angeles, California: National Conference of Christians and Jews, Asian-American Journalists Association and Association of Asian-Pacific American Artists, 1989.

Takaki, Ronald. *Strangers from a Different Shore: A History of Asian Americans.* Boston: Little, Brown and Company, 1989.

Uchida, Yoshiko. *Desert Exile: The Uprooting of a Japanese American Family.* Seattle, Washington: University of Washington Press, 1982.

United States Commission on Civil rights. *Civil Rights Issues Facing Asian Americans in the 1990s.* Washington, D.C., 1992.

Fiction, Poetry

Kingston, Maxine Hong. *Woman Warrior.* New York: Vintage Books, 1977.

Larsen, Wendy and Nga Tran Thi. *Shallow Graves: Two Women and Vietnam.* New York: Random House, 1986.

Lord, Bette B. *In the Year of the Boar and Jackie Robinson.* New York: Harper and Row, 1974.

Mori, Toshio. *Yokohama, California*. Seattle, Washington: University of Washington Press, 1949.

Sone, Monica. *Nisei Daughter*. Seattle, Washington: University of Washington Press, 1979.

Snyder, Dianne. *The Boy of the Three-Year Nap*. Boston: Houghton Mifflin, 1988.

Tan, Amy. *Joy Luck Club*. New York: Putnam, 1989.

Uchida, Yoshiko. *The Best Bad Thing*. New York: Macmillan, 1983.

Uchida, Yoshiko. *The Two Foolish Cats*. Margaret K. McElderry Books, 1987.

Yee, Paul. *Tales from Gold Mountain: Stories of the Chinese in the New World*. New York: Macmillan, 1990.

Young, Ed. *High on a Hill: A Book of Chinese Riddles*. New York: Harper Collins, 1980.

Folktales, Myths

Bang, Betsy. *The Demons of Rajpur: Five Tales from Bengal*. New York: Greenwillow, 1980.

Bang, Molly, *The Paper Crane*. New York: Greenwillow, 1985.

Bang, Molly Garrett. *Tye May and the Magic Brush*. New York: Greenwillow, 1981.

Bryan, Ashley. *Sh-Ko and His Eight Wicked Brothers*. New York: Atheneum, 1988.

Ginsburg, Mirra. *The Chinese Mirror: A Korean Folktale*. San Diego, California: Gulliver Books/Harcourt Brace Jovanovich, 1988.

Hamada, Cheryl. *The Farmer, The Buffalo, and the Tiger*. Chicago: Childrens Press, 1993.

Hamada, Cheryl. *The Fourth Question*. Chicago: Childrens Press, 1993.

Hamada, Cheryl. *The White Hare of Inaba*. Chicago: Childrens Press, 1993.

He, Liyi. *The Spring of Butterflies and Other Folktales of China's Minority Peoples*. Ed. Neil Philip. New York: Lothrop, Lee and Shepard, 1987.

Ishii, Momoko. *The Tongue-Cut Sparrow*. New York: Lodestar/E. P. Dutton, 1987.

Leaf, Margaret. *Eyes of the Dragon*. New York: Lothrop, Lee and Shepard, 1987.

Lee, Jeanne M. *Toad Is the Uncle of Heaven: A Vietnamese Folk Tale*. New York: Holt, Rinehart and Winston, 1985.

Louie, Ai-Ling. *Yeh-Shen: A Cinderella Story from China*. New York: Philomel, 1982.

Punpattanakul-Crouch, Wilai. *Kao and the Golden Fish*. Chicago: Childrens Press, 1993.

Vuong, Lynette Dyer. *The Brocaded Slipper and Other Vietnamese Tales*. Reading, Massachusetts: Addison-Wesley, 1982.

Yep, Laurence. *The Rainbow People*. New York: Harper and Row, 1989.

Xiong, Blia. *Nine-In-One Grr! Grr!: A Folktale from the Hmong People of Laos*. Emeryville, California: Children's Book Press, 1989.

Yolen, Jane. *The Emperor and the Kite*. Cleveland, Ohio: World Publishing, 1967.

Videos/Films

American Eyes. Produced by Cynthia A. Cherbak Productions. Distributed by Media Guild, San Francisco, California, 1990. (Korean)

American Success Stories: Yue-Sai Kan. Produced by Encyclopaedia Britannica Educational Corp. Chicago, Illinois, 1989. (Chinese)

Asian Insight Series. Produced by Film Australia. Dist. by Films Inc. Video. Chicago, Illinois, 1986. (General Asian)

Asians in America. Produced by Jade Productions. Distributed by Barr Films. Irwindale, California, 1986. (Vietnamese)

The Asianization of America. Produced by Films for the Humanities and Sciences, Princeton, New Jersey, 1988. (General Asian)

Becoming American. Ken Levine. Available from Iris Films. Seattle, Washigton. (Hmong)

Between Two Worlds. Produced by Siegel Productions. Distributed by Film Ideas, Northbrook, Illinois, 1986. (Laotian/Cambodian)

The Boy Who Drew Cats. Produced by Rabbit Ears Productions. Distributed by Uni. Universal City, California, 1991. (Japanese)

China: Land of My Father. Produced by Disney Educational Prods. Distributed by Coronet/MTI., Deerfield, Illinois, 1985. (Chinese)

Chinese Gold. Produced by Chip Taylor Communications. Derry, New Hampshire, 1988. (Chinese)

Dollar a Day, Ten Cents a Dance. Produced by Cinema Guild. New York, 1985. (Filipino)

Family Gathering. Produced by New Day Films. New York, 1988. (Japanese)

Inside Stories: Dance to Remember. Produced by Toronto Talkies. Distributed by Beacon Films. Evanston, Illinois, 1991. (Japanese)

Mother Tongue. Produced by TV Ontario. Distributed by TVO Video. Chapel Hill, North Carolina, 1992. (Vietnamese)

Moving Mountains. Produced by Filmakers Library, New York, 1990. (Laotian/Cambodian)

My Mother Thought She Was Audrey Hepburn. Produced by Filmakers Library. New York, 1991. (Chinese)

A Nation of Immigrants: 1805-1990. Produced by Agency for Instructional Technology, Bloomington, Indiana, 1991. (General Asian)

Isamu Noguchi. Produced by Home Vision. Chicago, Illinois, 1989. (Japanese)

Ozawa. Produced by Cami Video. Distributed by Kultur Video. West Long Branch, New Jersey, 1985. (Japanese)

Peachboy. Produced by Rabbit Ears Productions. Distributed by Uni. Universal City, California, 1991. (Japanese)

Rebuilding the Temple: Cambodians in America. Produced by Direct Cinema. Los Angeles, California, 1992. (Cambodian)

A Sari Tale. Produced by TV Ontario. Distributed by TVO Video. Chapel Hill, North Carolina, 1992. (South Asian Indian)

Tapestry II. Produced by Organization of Asian Women. Distributed by Third World Newsreel, New York, 1991. (General Asian)

Thanh's War. Produced by University of California Extension Media Center), 1991. (Vietnamese)

The Tiger and the Rahmin. Produced by Rabit Ears Prods. Distributed by Uni. Universal City, California, 1991. (South Asian Indian)

Unfinished Business. Produced by Mouchette Films. San Francisco, California, 1985. (Japanese)

Visible Target. Produced by Wombat Film & Video/Altschul Group, Evanston, Illinois, 1986. (Japanese)

Index

A

Acting careers
  Ahn, Philip, 124-127
  Hayakawa, Sessue
    (Kintaro), 92-95
  Lee, Bruce, 188-190
  Wong, Anna May,
    111-113
Aerospace engineers.
  See also Astronauts
  Onizuka, Ellison S.,
    206-210
AFL-CIO, 47
Ahn, Chang-Ho, 124-127
Ahn, Philip, 124-127
Aiken, Howard, 145
Akiyoshi, Toshiko,
  168-169
Alien land laws, 10
"Aloha Oe," 57
America Is in the Heart
  (Bulosan), 66-67
American Can Company,
  162
American Drug-Free
  Powerlifting Assoia-
  tion (ADFPA), 246
American Institute of
  Architects, 136, 141
Angel Island, prisoners
  of, 29-33
Aoki, Tsuru, 93
Aquino, Ninoy M., 71
Award, Philip Cruz as
  winner of, in 1987,
  71
Architects
  Lin, Maya Ying,
    236-238
  Pei, I. M., 140-143
  Yamasaki, Minoru,
    135-136
Archivists
  Cordova, Dorothy,
    186-187
  Cordova, Fred,
    186-187
Artists. *See also*
  Sculptors
  Aruego, Jose,
    170-172
  Kingman, Doug,
    127-129
  Obata, Chiura, 73-75
  Paik, Nam June,
    201-203
  Say, Allen, 178-179
  Wong, Jade Snow,
    150-152
Aruego, Jose, 170-172
Aruego, Juan, 171

B

Asian Pacific Americans,
  9
  immigration of, 9-13
Asia Pacific Triangle, 12
Aspen Music Festival,
  247
Astronauts
  Onizuka, Ellison S.,
    206-210
  Trinh, Eugene H.,
    239-240
Athletes. *See* Sports
  figures
AT&T, 147
Authors. *See* Writers
Autobiographies
  *America Is in the
    Heart* (Bulosan),
    66-67
  East Goes West
    (Kang), 109
  Grass Roof
    (Kang), 109
  *Hawaii's Story by
    Hawaii's Queen*
    (Liliuokalani), 57
  *My Life in China and
    in America* (Wing), 27
  Awakening of Faith
    (Suzuki), 69
Awamura, Margaret
  Shinobu, 155

B

Bandleaders. *See also*
  Musicians
  Akiyoshi, Toshiko,
    168-169
  King, Charles
    Edward, 58-59
Bank of China (Hong
  Kong), 142, 143
Bao, Cathy, 180
Bao, Dora, 180
Bao, Sandys, 180
Bao, San-san, 180, 181
"Batman" (television
  series), 188
Battle Hymn (film), 125,
  126
Battle Zone (film), 126
Bemis, Charlie, 40-41
Bemis, Polly (Lalu
  Nathoy), 39-42
Berkshire Music Center,
  174
Bernstein, Leonard, 174
Best Bad Things
  (Uchida), 99
Beyond Words (Obata),
  75

Birthday Visitor
  (Uchida), 96, 99
Black lung disease, 166
Bombay String Quartet,
  176
Borglum, Gutzon, 101
Boston Symphony
  Orchestra, 175, 176
Boulez, Pierre, 177
*Boy of the Three Year
  Nap* (Snyder), 178,
  179
Brancusi, Constantin,
  101
Bridge on the River Kwai
  (film), 94
Brother My Brother
  (Santos), 131
Bulosan, Aurelio, 66
Bulosan, Carlos, 64-67
Bunting, Eve, 179
Business people
  Shoong, Joe as,
    46-48
  Singh, Sirdar Jagjit,
    120-121
  Tsai, Gerard, Jr.,
    161-162

C

Cage, John, 202
Cambodian-Americans
  Pran, Dith, 191-195
  Yin, Luoth, 196-197
Cambodian refugees, 12
Canton, China, 15
Carus, Paul, 68
Casablanca, 105
Cellar, Emmanuel, 121
Central Pacific Railroad,
  21-22
Century Plaza Complex
  (Los Angeles), 136
Ceramicists. *See also*
  Artists
  Wong, Jade Snow,
    150-152
Chai Ha Lum, 117
Chang, Joe, 250-251
Chang, Michael, 250-251
Chan Is Missing (film),
  215
*Charge of the Light
  Brigade,* 105
Charleston Gazette, 166
*Chauvinist and Other
  Stories* (Mori), 123
Chavez, Cesar, 71
Chennault, Anna
  (Sheng Mai),
  156-157

Chennault, Claire Lee,
  157
Chiao Tung University,
  145
Chicago Symphony
  Orchestra's Ravinia
  Festival, 174
Child of the Owl (Yep),
  211
China Men (Kingston),
  185
China-Toggery-Shoong
  Company, 46
Chinatown, 35-38
  in New York City, 35
  in San Francisco,
    16, 21, 31, 35
Chinese Academy of
  Science, 134
Chinese-Americans
  Bemis, Polly (Lalu
    Nathoy), 39-42
  Chang, Michael,
    250-251
  Chennault, Anna
    (Sheng Mai),
    156-157
  Chuen, Lee Hoi, 188
  Chung, Connie,
    209-210
  Howe, James Wong,
    104-106
  Hwang, David
    Henry, 224-226
  Kingman, Doug,
    127-129
  Kingston, Maxine
    Hong, 183-185
  as laundry workers,
    43-45
  Lee, Bruce, 188-190
  Lee, Tsung Dao,
    158-160
  Lord, Bette Bao,
    180-182
  Ma, Yo-Yo, 222-223
  Ozawa, Seiji,
    173-176
  Pei, I. M., 140-143
  as railroad workers,
    21-23
  Shoong, Joe, 46-48
  as sugar cane
    workers in Hawaii,
    49-52
  Tan, Amy, 217-218
  Tsai, Gerard, Jr.,
    161-162
  Wang, An, 144-147
  Wang, Wayne,
    215-216

Wing, Yung, 24-27
Wong, Anna May, 111-113
Wong, Jade Snow, 150-152
Wu, Chien Shiung, 132-134
Yang, Chen Ning, 158-160
Yep, Lawrence, 211-212
Chinese Consolidated Benevolent Associations, 35-38
Chinese Exclusion Acts (1882), 10, 29
  repeal of, 33
Chinese immigration, 10, 29, 33
Chinese ladies garment workers, 47
Chinese Six Companies, 16, 17, 35-38
Chinese Sky (movie), 126
Ching, Tao Te, 68
Chung, Connie, 209-210
Chung, Kyung-Wha, 220
Chung, Myung-So, 220
Chung, Myung-Wha, 220
Chung, Myung-Whun, 219-221
Chung, Sunyol, 220
Church Fruits, 199
Cinematographers. *See also* Acting careers
  Howe, James Wong, 104-106
Civil Air Transport (CAT), 157
Civil Liberties Act (1988), 87
Civil Rights Memorial, 238
CNA, 162
Coaches. *See also* Sports figures
  Lee, Sammy, 148-149
Columbia University, 69, 133, 134, 136, 158, 159, 160, 239
Come Back, Little Sheba, 105
Commission on Wartime Relocation and Internment of Civilians (CWRIC), 83
Commodity Futures Trading Commission, 205
Community leaders
  Cordova, Dorothy,

186-187
  Cordova, Fred, 186-187
  Yin, Luoth, 196-197
Composers. *See also* Musicians
  King, Charles Edward, 58-59
  Paik, Nam June, 201-203
Computer wizards
  Wang, An, 144-147
Conductors. *See also* Musicians
  Chung, Myung-Whun, 219-221
  Mehta, Zubin, 176-177
  Ozawa, Seiji, 173-176
Confucius, 15
Congressional Commission on Wartime Relocation and Internment of Civilians, 85
Conservation of parity law, 158-159
Consulate, U.S. (Kobe, Japan), 136
Cordova, Dorothy, 186-187
Cordova, Fred, 186-187
Crawford, Joan, 105
Crocker, Charles, 21, 22
Cruz, Phillip Vera, 70-72

D
Dallas City Hall, 141
Dance and the Railroad (Hwang), 225
Dao, Yang, 235
Daughter of Fu Manchu (film), 112
Daughter of Shanghai (film), 112
Daughter of the Dragon (film), 112
Deltamax cores, 146
DeMille, Cecil B., 93
Demostration Project for Asian Americans, 187
Desert Exile, 99
Dewey, Ariane, 170-171
De Witt, John L., 85
Dietrich, Marlene, 105
Dim Sum (film), 216
Diplomats
  Wing, Yung, 24
Doctors
  Lee, Sammy, 148-149

Dole, Sanford B., 57
Doll, Clyde, 245-246
Dragon of the Lost Sea (Yep), 211
Dragonwings (Yep), 211

E
East Goes West (Kang), 109
Eat a Bowl of Tea (film), 216
Echo of our Song: Chants and Poems of the Hawaiians (Pukui), 61
Economists
  Gramm, Wendy Lee, 204-205
Editors. *See also* Writers
  Pukui, Mary Kawena, 60-61
Educators
  Hayakawa, Samuel Ichiye, 114-116
  Kang, Younghill, 109-110
  Kingston, Maxine Hong, 183-185
  Obata, Chiura, 73-75
  Suzuki, D. T., 68-69
  Wing, Yung, 24
  Wu, Chien Shiung, 132-134
Eighth Moon (Lord), 181
Emma, Queen, 58-59
Enter the Dragon (film), 190
Essays in Zen Buddhism (Suzuki), 69
Everson Museum, 141
Executive Order 9066, 77, 87, 89, 96

F
Fairbanks, Douglas, 93, 111
Family Red Apple store, 199
Famous Artist's School, 129
Feast of Lanterns (Say), 179
Federal Trade Commission, 205
Fidelity Fund, 161
Fifth Chinese Daughter (Wong), 150, 152
Figure skaters
  Yamaguchi, Kristi, 252-253
Filipino American Historical Society, 187

Filipino-Americans
  Aruego, Jose, 170-172
  Bulosan, Carlos, 64-67
  Cordova, Dorothy, 186-187
  Cordova, Fred, 186-187
  Cruz, Phillip Vera, 70-72
  Manlapit, Pablo, 62-63
  Santos, Bienvenido N., 130-131
  as sugar cane workers in Hawaii, 49-52
Filipino Federation of Labor, 63
Filipino Higher Wage Movement, 63
Filipino labor union, 63, 67
Film directors
  Wang, Wayne, 215-216
Financiers
  Tsai, Gerard, Jr., 161-162
Fists of Fury (film), 190
Fletcher School of Law and Diplomacy, 181
Flower Drum Song (film), 129
F.O.B. (Hwang), 225
Folk Tales from Hawaii (Pukui and Green), 60
Fong, Hiram, 117-119
Fong, Lum, 117
Foot binding, 39
Ford, Gerald, 87, 157
Forrester, Dr., 146
442nd Combat Regiment, in World War II, 80, 89-91, 138, 154
Fourteenth Amendment, 10
Freedom Forum, 182
Friendship Society, 124
Fu Manchu movies, 112

G
Galindo, Rudi, 253
General Died at Dawn (film), 125
Gila, Arizona, Japanese-American detention camp in, 78
Gilmour, Leonie, 100
Githens and Keally

(architectural firm), 135-136
Gold Mountain, travelers to, 15-19
Good Earth (film), 112, 125
Goto, Setsu, 247
Government officials. *See* Diplomats; House of Representative members; Senators
Gramm, Phil, 204-205
Gramm, Wendy Lee, 204-205
Granada, Colorado, Japanese-American detention camp in, 78
Grandfather's Journey (Say), 179
Grass Root (Kang), 109
Green, Laura, 60
"Green Hornet" (television series), 188

H

Halls of Montezuma (film), 126
Hanapepe Massacre, 63
Happiest Ending (Uchida), 99
Harvard Computation Laboratory, 145
Harvard University, 145, 223
School of Design, 140-141
Hawaii, sugar cane workers in, 49-52, 54, 62, 63
Hawaiian Association of American Ministers, 54
Hawaiians
King, Charles Edward, 58-59
Liliuokalani, Lydia, 56-57
Malo, Davida, 53-55
Matsunaga, Masayuki "Spark," 138-139
Mink, Patsy Takemoto, 163-164
Onizuka, Ellison S., 206-210
Pukui, Mary Kawena, 60-61
Hawaiian Antiquities (Malo), 53, 55
Hawaiian Dictionary and

Place Names of Hawaii (Pukui), 61
Hawaiian Folk Tales (Pukui), 61
Hawaiian Stories and Wise Sayings (Pukui and Green), 60
Hawaiian Sugar Planter's Association, 62, 63
Hawaii's Story by Hawaii's Queen (Liliuokalani), 57
Hayakawa, Samuel Ichiye, 114-116
Hearst, William Randolph, 121
Heart Mountain, Wyoming, Japanese-American detention camp in, 78
Heifitz, Jascha, 248
"He Mele Lahui Hawaii," 57
Hewlett-Packard, 147
Hirabayashi, Gordon, 85, 86, 87
Hiroshima (band), 213-214
Hmong refugees, 233-235
Hoang, Phuong, 227-228
Hong, Ying Lan, 183
Hong Kong, 15
Hopkins, Mark, 21
Horner, Jill, 223
House of Representative members. *See also* Senators
Gramm, Phil, 204-205
Mink, Patsy Takemoto, 163-164
Saund, Dalip Singh, 107-110
Howe, James Wong, 104-106
Hud (film), 105
Hula, 60
Huntington, Collis P., 21
Hwang, David Henry, 224-226

I

IBM, 147
Illinois Institute of Technology, 114
Illustrators. *See also* Artists
Aruego, Jose, 170-172
Say, Allen, 178-179

Imanaga, Kame, 153
Immigration, Asian Pacific American, 9-13
Immigration Act (1917), 10-11
Immigration Act (1924), 109
Immigration and Nationality Act, 1965 amendments to, 12
Immigration and Naturalization Act (1952), 12
Immigration Reform and Control Act (1986), 13
India Arts and Crafts, 121
India League of America, 121
Indian-Americans
Mehta, Zubin, 176-177
Saund, Dalip Singh, 107-110
Singh, Sirdar Jagjit, 120-121
Indian Association of America, 108
Inn-Keeper's Apprentice (Say), 179
Inouye, Daniel K., 153-155
Inouye, Hyotaro, 153
Institute for Advanced Study (Princeton), 159, 160
Institute for Theoretical Physics (SUNY-Stony Brook), 160
Introduction to Zen Buddhism (Suzuki), 69
Iron Hand (film), 190
Israel Philharmonic, 177
Itliong, Larry, 70
Ito, Kohen, 135

J

Japanese American Citizens League (JACL), 77, 85, 86
Japanese American Evacuation Claims Act (1948), 87
Japanese-American internment camps, 73-75, 83, 85-86, 97-98, 102, 123
Japanese-Americans
Akiyoshi, Toshiko,

168-169
Hayakawa, Samuel Ichiye, 114-116
Hayakawa, Sessue (Kintaro), 92-95
Inouye, Daniel K., 153-155
Kang, Younghill, 109-110
Kuramoto, June, 213-214
Midori, 247-249
Mori, Toshio, 122-126
Noguchi, Isamu, 100-103
Obata, Chiura, 73-75
Say, Allen, 178-179
as sugar cane workers in Hawaii, 49-52
Suzuki, D.T., 68-69
Uchida, Yoshiko, 96-99
Yamaguchi, Kristi, 252-253
Yamasaki, Minoru, 135-136
Japanese Symphony Orchestra, 174
Jar of Dreams (Uchida), 99
Jerome, Arkansas, Japanese-American detention camp in, 78
JFK International Airport, 141
Journalists. *See* Reporters
Journey to Topaz, 99
Joy Luck Club (Tan), 218
Juan and the Asuangs (Aruego), 171
Juillard School of Music, 220, 247, 248

K

Kalukua, David, 56
Kang, Younghill, 109-110
Kellogg, Mary, 25-26
Kennedy, John F., Memorial Library, 141
Khmer News, 197
Killing Fields (film), 194
King, Charles Edward, 58-59
King, Hong, 40
King and His Friends (Aruego), 171
Kingman, Doug, 127-129
King's Book of Hawaiian

Melodies, 59

Kingsport Times and News (Tennessee), 166

King's Songs of Hawaii, 59

Kingston, Earll, 184

Kingston, Joseph, 184

Kingston, Maxine Hong, 183-185, 224

Kipling, Rudyard, 120-121

Kitchen God's Wife (Tan), 217

Kjarsgaard, Christy, 252

Kogun (album), 169

Korean-Americans
Ahn, Chang-Ho, 124-127
Ahn, Philip, 124-127
Chung, Myung-Whun, 219-221
Gramm, Wendy Lee, 204-205
in grocery and convenience store business, 199-200
Lee, K. W., 165-167
Lee, Sammy, 148-149
Paik, Nam June, 201-203
as sugar cane workers in Hawaii, 49-52

Korean National Association, 124

Korea Times, 167

Koreatown Weekly, 167-168

Korematsu, Fred, 85, 86, 87

Korn, Alfons K., 61

"Kung Fu" (television series), 126, 188

Kuramoto, Dan, 213-214

Kuramoto, June, 213-214

Ky, Hguyen Cao, 229-230

L

Labor leaders
Cruz, Phillip Vera, 70-72
Manlapit, Pablo, 62-63

Labor unions
Chinese Ladies Garment Workers as, 47
Filipino Labor Union as, 63, 67
Filipino Federation of Labor as, 63

United Farm Workers as, 71

Language in Thought and Action (Hayakawa), 114

Laos, Hmong refugees from, 233-235

Laughter of My Father (Bulosan), 66

Laundry business, Chinese, 43-45

Lawrence, Ernest, 132

Lee, Bruce, 188-190

Lee, Chol Soo, 166

Lee, K. W., 165-167

Lee, Sammy, 242

Lee, Tsung Dao, 133, 158-160

Legacies: A Chinese Mosaic (Lord), 182

Legends of Kawaelo (Pukui and Green), 60

Leonard, Andy, 244-246

Leonard, Richard, 245

Leo the Late Bloomer (Aruego), 171

Letter from America (Bulosan), 66

Life Is Cheap...but Toilet Paper is Expensive (film), 216

Liliuokalani, Lydia, 56-57, 58

Lin, Maya Ying, 236-238

Lincoln, Abraham, 21

Literacy tests, 10

Little Saigon, 230-231

Liverpool International Conductor's Competition, 176

Loo, Eileen, 140-141

Look What I Can Do, Oliver (Aruego), 171

Lord, Bette Bao, 180-182

Lord, Winston, 180-182

Los Angeles Art Center School, 178

Los Angeles Philharmonic, 177

Los Angeles Symphony, 220

Louganis, Despina, 241

Louganis, Frances, 241

Louganis, Greg, 149, 241-243

Louganis, Peter, 241

Louvre Museum, 141-142

Love Is a Many Splendored Thing (film), 125

Luce, Clare Boothe, 121

Lucky Yak (Bunting), 179

Lunalilo, William, 58

M

Ma, Hiao-Tsiun, 222

Ma, Marina, 222

Ma, Yeou-Cheng, 222

Ma, Yo-Yo, 222-223

Macao, 24

Magic and the Night River (Bunting), 179

Malo, A'alaioa (daughter), 55

Malo, A'alaioa (wife), 53

Malo, Davida, 53-55

Malo, Lepeka (Rebecca), 54-55

Malo, Pahia, 54

Mangaoang, Ernesto, 70

Manhattan Fund, 162

Manlapit, Pablo, 62-63

Manzanar, California, Japanese-American detention camp in, 78

Marcos, Ferdinand, 131

Mariano, Charlie, 168

Mark I, 145

Martial artists
Lee, Bruce, 188-190

Massachusetts Institute of Technology (MIT), 140

Matsunaga, Spark, 164

M Butterfly (Hwang), 224, 225

McAuliffe, Christa, 207

McCarran-Walter Act (1952), 105-106

Mehta, Zubin, 176-177

Mensalves, Chris, 70, 71

Menuhin, Yehudi, 248

Merchants
Singh, Sirdar Jagjit, 120-121

Miao, Cora, 215

Midori, 247-249

Mingus, Charles, 168

Minidoka, Idaho, Japanese-American detention camp in, 78

Mink, Gwendolyn, 163

Mink, John, 163

Mink, Patsy Takemoto, 138, 163-164

Mitterand, Francois, 141

Montreal Symphony, 177

Mori, Toshio, 122-126

Mountain of Gold (Sung), 16-19

Mount Rushmore

National Memorial, 101

Movie careers. See Acting careers; Cinematographers; Film directors

Mudd, Roger, 210

Musicians
Akiyoshi, Toshiko, 168-169
Chung, Myung-Whun, 219-221
King, Charles Edward, 58-59
Kuramoto, June, 213-214
Liliuokalani, Lydia, 56-57
Ma, Yo-Yo, 222-223
Mehta, Zubin, 176-177
Midori, 247-249
Ozawa, Seiji, 173-176
Paik, Nam June, 201-203

Mutual Assistance Society, 124

My Life in China and in America (Wing), 27

N

"Na Lei O Hawai'i," 59

Nathoy, Lalu, 39-42

National Academy of Sciences, 133

National Center for Atmospheric Research, 141

National Central University, 132

National Dollar Stores, 46-47

Newport Jazz Festival, 169

News anchors. See also Reporters
Chung, Connie, 209-210

New York Philharmonic Orchestra, 174, 177

Ngor, Haing, 194

NHK Symphony, 174

Ni, Xiong, 241

Nixon, Richard, 154, 157

Nobel Prize in Physics
Chen Ning Yang as recipient of, 133, 160
Tsung Dao Lee as recipient of, 133, 160

Noguchi, Isamu, 100-103

Garden Museum,
103
Northwestern
University, 204

O

Obata, Chiura, 73-75
Obata, Haruko, 75
Office of Management
and Budget (OMB),
205
Old Man and the Sea,
105
Oliver, Sir Laurence,
112
Olympic participants
Chang, Michael,
250-251
Lee, Sammy,
148-149
Leonard, Andy,
244-246
Louganis, Greg,
241-243
Yamaguchi, Kristi,
252-253
*Once Under the Cherry
Blossom Tree* (Say),
179
Onizuka, Darien, 206
Onizuka, Janelle, 206
Onizuka, Ellison S.,
206-210
Open Court Publishing,
68
Opera de la Bastille,
220-221
Oppenheimer, Robert,
133
Otani University, 69
Ozawa, Seiji, 173-176

P

Pacific Railroad Act, 21
Paik, Nam June,
201-203
Painters. *See* Artists
Park, Man Ho, 199
Parsons School of
Design, 170
Pei, Chien Chung
("Didi"), 141
Pei, I. M., 140-143
Pei, Liane, 141
Pei, Li Chung
("Sandi"), 141
Pei, Ting Chung, 141
Pei Partnership, 142
Perkins, Maxwell, 110
Philanthropists
Shoong, Joe, 46-48
Philippine Islands, 49.

See also Filipino-
Americans
Philippines, University
of the, 170
Philosophers
Suzuki, D.T., 68-69
Photographers
Say, Allen, 178-179
Physicists
Lee, Tsung Dao,
158-160
Trinh, Eugene H.,
239-240
Wu, Chien Shiung,
132-134
Yang, Chen Ning,
158-160
Pickford, Mary, 93
Pioneers
Bemis, Polly (Lalu
Nathoy), 39-42
Playwrights. *See also*
Writers
Hwang, David
Henry, 224-226
Political activists
Chennault, Anna
(Sheng Mai),
156-157
Singh, Sirdar Jagjit,
120-121
Poston, Arizona,
Japanese-American
detention camp in,
78, 102-103
Pran, Dith, 191-195
Prejudice, against Asian
immigrants, 10, 12,
18-19
Presidential Proclama-
tion 4417, 87
Primerica, 162
Prince of Hawaii
(opera), 59
Princeton University,
133
Professional Children's
School, 247-248
Publishers
King, Charles
Edward, 58-59

R

Radio Symphony
Orchestra, 220
Rainier Square (Seattle),
136
Rather, Dan, 210
Ravinia Festival, 174
Reagan, Ronald, 83, 139
Red Lantern (film), 111
Refugees
Cambodian, 12

Hmong, 233-235
Vietnamese, 12,
227-232
Reporters
Chung, Connie,
209-210
Lee, K. W., 165-167
Pran, Dith, 191-195
Rhee, Syngman, 124
Richards, William, 54
Rockefeller Center, 101
Rohmer, Sax, 112
Rohwer, Arkansas,
Japanese-American
detention camp in,
78
Roosevelt, Franklin D.,
77, 89, 102, 121, 163
Rose Tattoo (film), 105
Royal Hawaiian Band, 59
Royal Liverpool
Philharmonic, 176
Rulers
Liliuokalani, Lydia,
56-57
Rumley, Edward, A.,
100-101

S

St. Louis Airport
Terminal Building,
136
Samurai of Gold Hill
(Uchida), 99
Sanford University,
224-225
San Francisco
Angel Island in,
29-33
Chinatown in, 16,
21, 31, 35-36
earthquakes in, 31,
46
San Francisco Art
Institute, 179
San Francisco State
University, 115
San Francisco
Symphony, 174-175
Santos, Bienvenido N.,
130-131
Saroyan, William, 122,
123
Saund, Dalip Singh,
107-110
Say, Allen, 178-179
Scent of Apples (Santos),
130, 131
Schanberg, Sydney,
191-195
Scientists
Lee, Tsung Dao,
158-160

Onizuka, Ellison S.,
206-210
Trinh, Eugene H.,
239-240
Wu, Chien Shiung,
132-134
Yang, Chen Ning,
158-160
Sculptors. *See also*
Artists
Lin, Maya Ying,
236-238
Noguchi, Isamu,
100-103
Sea Glass (Yep), 211
Senators. *See also*
House of Represen-
tative members
Fong, Hiram,
117-119
Hayakawa, Samuel
Ichiye, 114-116
Inouye, Daniel K.,
153-155
Matsunaga,
Masayuki "Spark,"
138-139
Shee, Lew, 127
Sheng Mai. *See*
Chennault, Anna
(Sheng Mai)
Shinpet, Noro, 178
Shoong, Joe, 46-48
Sihanouk, Norodom,
191
Singh, Sirdar Jagjit,
120-121
Six Companies, 16, 17,
35-38
Snyder, Dianne, 179
Social activists
Ahn, Chang-Ho,
124-127
Social service workers
Yin, Luoth, 196-197
Southern Poverty Law
Center, 238
Special Olympics,
245-246
Sports figures
Chang, Michael,
250-251
Lee, Sammy,
148-149
Leonard, Andy,
244-246
Louganis, Greg,
241-243
Yamaguchi, Kristi,
252-253
Spring Moon (Lord), 181
Stanford, Leland, 21
Star Fisher (Yep), 212

Sudden Unexplained
    Death Syndrome
    (SUDS), 234
Sugar cane workers,
    49-52, 54, 62, 63
Sung, Betty Lee, 16
Suzuki, D.T., 68-69
Swanson, Gloria, 105
Sweetwater (Yep), 211

T

Tabackin, Lew, 169
Tan, Amy, 217-218
Tan, Dora, 217
Tanforan,
    Assembly Center,
    San Bruno,
    California,
    Japanese-American
    detention camp at,
    74, 97
Teachers. *See* Educators
"Television Hula," 59
Temperance Society of
    Lahaima, 54
Tennis players
    Chang, Michael,
    250-251
Texas A & M University,
    204-205
Thief of Bagdhad (film),
    111-112
Toho Gakuen School of
    Music, 173
Tokyo Joe (film), 93
Tongs, 36-38
Topaz, Utah, Japanese-
    American detention
    camp in, 74-75, 78,
    98
Toronto Symphony
    Orchestra, 174
*Toshiko Akiyoshi: Jazz Is
    My Native Language*
    (film), 169
Translators
    Malo, Davida, 53-55
    Pukui, Mary
    Kawena, 60-61
Trinh, Yvette, 240
*Tripmaster Monkey: His
    Fake Book*
    (Kingston), 185
Truman, Harry, 91
Tsai, Gerard, Jr.,
    161-162
Tufts University, 181
Tule Lake, California,
    Japanese-American
    detention camp in,
    78
Tunney, John, 115
Typhoon (film), 93

U

Uchida, Kay, 97-98
Uchida, Yoshiko, 96-99
Unemployment, blame
    of, on Chinese
    workers, 22-23
Union Pacific Railroad,
    21-22
United Chinese Society,
    35
United Farm Workers,
    71
University of California
    at Berkeley, 107,
    179, 184, 212
University
    of California at Los
    Angeles Asian
    American Studies
    Center, 123
University of Hawaii,
    138, 153-154
University of Pennsylva-
    nia at Philadelphia,
    140
University of Tokyo, 201
University of Wisconsin
    at Madison, 114
Uranium fission, 132-134
Urban Redevelopment
    Plan (St. Louis), 136

V

Video painting, 203
Vietnamese-Americans
    Leonard, Andy,
    244-246
    Lin, Maya Ying,
    236-238
    Trinh, Eugene H.,
    239-240
Vietnamese refugees, 12,
    227-231
Vietnam Veterans
    Memorial, 236-238
Villa Magdalena
    (Santos), 131
Voice of Bataan
    (Bulosan), 66

W

Wang, An, 144-147
Wang, Lorraine, 146
Wang, Wayne, 215-216
Wang Center for
    Performing Arts,
    147
Wang Laboratories, 146,
    147
War Brides Act (1945),
    12
Warrens, Idaho
    Polly Bemis, 39-42
Washington, George,
    University Law
    School, 154
Wayne, John, 126
Weightlifters. *See also*
    Sports figures
    Leonard, Andy,
    244-246
Wellesley College, 204
Whitney Museum of
    American Art, 203
Whose Mouse Are You
    (Aruego), 171
Wichita State University,
    131
Wing, Yung, 24-27
Wolfe, Thomas, 110
*Woman Warrior:
    Memoirs of a
    Girlhood Among
    Ghosts* (Kingston),
    184-185
Wong, Anna May,
    111-113
Wong, Jade Snow,
    150-152
World Jazz Festival,
    169
World of Suzie Wong
    (film), 129
World Trade Center
    Towers (New York),
    135, 136, 137
World War II
    442nd Combat
    Regiment in, 80, 89-
    91, 138, 154
    internment of
    Japanese-
    Americans during,
    73-83, 85-86, 97-98,
    102, 123
Writers
    Bulosan, Carlos,
    64-67
    Cordova, Fred,
    186-187
Hwang, David
    Henry, 224-226
Kang, Younghill,
    109-110
Kingston, Maxine
    Hong, 183-185
Lord, Bette Bao,
    180-182
Malo, Davida, 53-55
Mori, Toshio,
    122-126
Pukui, Mary
    Kawena, 60-61
Santos, Bienvenido
    N., 130-131
Tan, Amy, 217-218
Uchida, Yoshiko,
    96-99
Wong, Jade Snow,
    150-152
Yep, Lawrence,
    211-212
Wu, Chien Shiung, 132-
    134, 159

Y

Yale University, 25, 236,
    238, 239
    School of Drama,
    225
Yamaguchi, Carole, 252
Yamaguchi, Jim, 252
Yamaguchi, Kristi,
    252-253
Yamaguchi, Yoshiko
    (Shirley), 103
Yamasaki, Minoru,
    135-136
Yang, Chen Ning, 133,
    158-160
Yankee Doodle Dandy,
    105
Yasui, Minoru, 85, 86, 87
*Year of the Boar and
    Jackie Robinson*
    (Lord), 181
Yep, Lawrence, 211-212
Yin, Luoth, 196-197
Yokohama, California
    (Mori), 122
Yoshida, Lorna, 206
You Lovely People
    (Santos), 131

Z

Zen Buddhism, 68-69,
    94-95
Zukerman, Pinchas, 247

Picture Acknowledgments

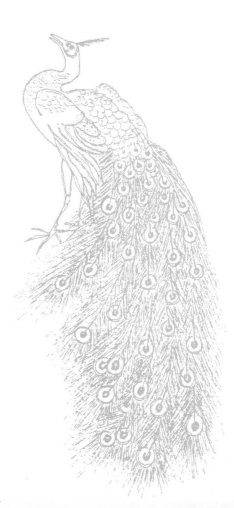

About the Author

Susan Sinnott began her publishing career as an editor for Cricket, a literary magazine for children. She later worked at the University of Wisconsin Press, where she managed and edited academic journals. Eventually, her own two children pulled her away from scholarly publishing and helped her rediscover the joys of reading and writing books for young people. Ms. Sinnott has written *Zebulon Pike, Jacques Cousteau, Dith Pran* (forthcoming), and *Extraordinary Hispanic Americans* for Childrens Press. She lives in Portsmouth, New Hampshire, with her husband and children.

About the Designer–Illustrator

Lindaanne Yee-Donohoe worked in fashion advertising and at an advertising art studio before embarking in publishing in 1986. As a free-lance designer–illustrator, she has worked for several book publishers. Currently, her creative talents are being utilized by Childrens Press, for whom she has designed and electronically produced several popular series: *Encyclopedia of Presidents, The World's Great Explorers,* and *Extraordinary People.* Ms. Donohoe lives in Chicago, Illinois, with her daughter Nicole.